The Source
Initiation into Love and Freedom

Tilicho

Arunachala Publication

Arunachala Publication,
Shanti Neelam, 606604 Adiannamalai, India.
ISBN 979-10-91141-01-7
EAN 9791091141017
Publication number: 979-10-91141
Legal registration: July 2012
Printed in July 2012 by Lulu Press International.
Cover illustration from a mural painted by Bella Wilshire and
photographed by Valentina Mengarelli in Deer Park (Bir, India).
Book illustrations: Lila, Marie and Tilicho.

To my "little" sources of love, Lila and Marie.

Table of Contents

Acknowledgements

I would like to express my gratitude to all the people who have been more or less involved in this adventure. I am particularly grateful to the friends who have offered their precious support as well as their help with the correction of the manuscript in French and English: Annamalai, Anne, Armand, Caroline, Charlotte, Jennifer, Jo-Yves, Ragi and Upahar. I am also very grateful to life for guiding me to Tiruvannamalai where I discovered the teaching of the sage Ramana Maharshi and heard other teachers.

I deeply thank my loving parents, my sister, my grandmother, all my family and also my late grandparents to whom I owe everything. I would also like to thank Khalis, Lila and Marie for their participation in this adventure.

Introduction

Lila, 5 years old.

Uma the octopus

Uma the octopus lived happily in the depths of the ocean softly rocked by the waves. One day, though, some of her tentacles stopped following the flow. Captivated by the illusion of being independent and separate, they forgot their unity and their true identity. Just like these tentacles, have we not forgotten who we really are?

Despite the mist of forgetfulness, our deeper self knows and calls us. Some name it God, Christ, Allah, Buddha, the Tao or Mother Nature. Some others call it *the Self, Pure Consciousness, the Source or the Heart.*[1] Different names are given, but they all point at the same one reality: the eternal Self, the unchanging essence of eternally changing forms.

We spend our lives seeking our original happiness. As we have mostly forgotten its flavour, we search for it in many directions and sometimes, we get lost. We may limit happiness to romantic love or material wealth. Even if love and wealth generally contribute to happiness, we also know that some people have both and yet feel inside that something is lacking. How can true happiness be found?

True happiness is the divine fragrance at the core of ourselves, the soft scent of a flower open in the sun and the rain. It is the eternal temple no wind can reclaim. The inner peace that is not dependent upon external conditions is our shelter and profound nature.

Some people consciously wish to rediscover this peace. They are called spiritual seekers. They lead a monastic life, follow spiritual teachings or engage in selfless deeds. For other people, there is no spiritual quest. They simply find inner peace by following the flow of life. All paths eventually lead to Self-realisation.[2] Whoever the people and their beliefs, the Self is already the Heart of our nature. Nobody is

---

[1] The names in italics are the ones that are generally used throughout the book. In this example, the Heart means Love.
[2] Inner peace and Self-knowledge.

excluded from it, nobody is far from it. The veil of forgetfulness simply needs to be removed.

Chapter 1: Spiritual Experience

"Nothing"

The ego may cling to spiritual experiences because they are unusual. This is why spiritual experiences should not be taken too seriously. However, it is natural to wish for clarity concerning them. This helps to free the mind from doubts and questions. In my case, I tried to obtain clear explanations for my experience but in vain. Therefore, I had to put aside my doubts in order to place my trust in my inner responses only. This took many years but finally, the doubts have stopped.

In 1998 my interests and occupations were not spiritual. I had not yet started doing yoga, I had not read any spiritual books and I did not subscribe to any religion or follow any spiritual teacher. I was living in France and I was leading an ordinary life which could be defined as an active and happy one. One day, I "heard" from within a loud "Stop!" I listened to this cry and I stopped everything in order to take time to do nothing, take walks in nature and be alone with myself. It was then that numerous dreams assailed me. In one of these dreams, a group of sages showed me some books. They were telling me that I ought to understand; but understand what exactly? An unexpected and incredible inner fire made me pounce upon a spiritual book to try to understand the meaning of life. I skimmed over the sentences at a mad speed. I searched for words which would speak to me, words which I could feel were truthful. It was not so much my reading but rather the "fire" in me and a painting on my wall that suddenly opened my eyes and allowed me to understand what my true nature *is*.

This painting was completely black and was called "Nothing". In the centre, a space was cut out of the canvas, so one could see right through. It turned out to be a revelation. Everything became so clear. I understood that as long as we do not know our true nature, we are like the blackness of the painting, prisoners of our ignorance. When we start to clearly see within ourselves, a space opens out, which allows us to see through and realise who we really are. Like this space, our true nature is independent of everything even though everything manifests in it. The world changes but this space is always the same and will remain the same, eternally. The more we clearly see within ourselves, the more ignorance diminishes. The inner space grows. When there is clarity, darkness disappears. Only the frame remains. This frame, which is symbolically the body, will pass away, but the space remains ever present. Who we truly are never dies.

When the mind is clear and open, there is only space. There is no separation from the true Self which has always been there, omnipresent, beyond time, without limits and without boundaries with all that *is*: One, absolutely One. This really was a revelation. The next day, while I was reading with the same intensity, I directly experienced my true nature: Pure Consciousness (Truth). Individual consciousness is often limited by wrong beliefs about its true identity. When this is no longer the case, and when the mind is open, the individual directly experiences who she/he really is. This experience is called enlightenment. Depending on the people, enlightenment leads more or less quickly to a state of wisdom and steady openness.

When the experience of enlightenment happens, ego dissolves at the cellular level (unconsciousness merges in the Light). However, mental habits can still be present. Metaphorically we can say: "The fan is switched off but it still spins for a while". This is beautifully described by Yvan Amar: "What is called enlightenment or illumination, stops radically, yet not immediately, the mechanism of behaviour based on self-interest. It requires years afterwards for this new way of being to manifest in daily life: not only at the level of the mind, where doubts transform into wisdom, and at the level of the heart, where anger transforms into compassion, but also at the level of the body, where fears transform into joy." [3]

So many myths and extraordinary stories are told about enlightenment that I could not totally believe, at the beginning, that my experience was enlightenment. When I innocently shared my point of view on spirituality and enlightenment with other people, it often

---

[3] Yvan Amar, *L'Effort et la Grâce*, Albin Michel, 2005, p.19.

8

ended in misunderstandings. Since nothing in me corresponded to the mythical image of an enlightened person, I was considered arrogant, pretentious or someone having problems. Finally, I decided to keep quiet, as harmony is often preferable to the expression of one's ideas, if they are not welcome. However, not expressing myself was also not natural. Over time, if the course of water is blocked, it may overflow. This is why I felt the need to write this book. I felt the need to freely express my opinion because I could see that spiritual idealism often turned people away from Truth.

When I started to write, my intention was simply to share my views on spirituality. I also wanted to share my awareness of the ego as clarity dissolves shadows. But writing this book became an adventure. In the process, I realised new things. First, I noticed how powerful words are when they come from the source of our Being. Strangely, what I was writing was manifesting into reality. This made me realise the responsibility I had in choosing words, examples and the way to realise the Self. By presenting all the different aspects of the ego, I also understood that this book could accelerate the process of Self-realisation. But was this acceleration safe? Finally, I realised that this acceleration could be beneficial and safe by integrating two paths: the outer path (experience of life and knowledge of ego) softened by the inner path (dissolution of ego by observation of "I" thoughts[4]). Given this understanding, this book can help you find inner peace and realise who you are.

---

[4] Ego manifests as "I" thoughts such as "I want", "I desire" and "I fear".

9

Chapter 2: Recognising Your True Nature

Lila, 8 years old.

Who Are You Truly?

It is important to understand your true nature because it lifts the veil of ignorance. As long as this veil is not removed, you are trapped by the appearance of forms and the illusion of separation. To lift the veil of ignorance is not complicated. It is not necessary to go into a deep intellectual study. You can lift this veil in many ways, the easiest ones being intuitive, introspective and visual.

Intuition

You can first understand your true nature through intuition and deduction. Sometimes, you have intuition. You feel what the weather will be like tomorrow, whether a job suits you or not, when it is a good time to call your friend and whether you should turn right or left on the road. You feel an inner Presence. There seems to be a clear voice within. Whose voice is this? It knows about you because it often appears as a personal guide, an intuitive counsellor. Does this inner guide know only about you? No. If it gives you advice about the outside world it is because it also has knowledge of the outer reality: the road to take, the job that is right for you and the solution to your problems.

Is this voice within you only? It is clear that animals are also in touch with their inner voice. In the case of the 2004 tsunami, reports have shown that they must have anticipated the disaster and so escaped. Animals are generally more intuitive than human beings. We also know that plants have a certain knowledge. They are sensitive to music, love, voices and the atmosphere that surrounds them. From these examples, we can deduce that in every organism, there is a greater consciousness that is not limited to a physical body.

Who are you then? Are you only your body? Or are you this consciousness that is greater than your body and permeates everything? Each individual has a physical form but there is, evidently, a greater "body". This body is not visible to the eyes but it

13

is real. Because it knows, we can call it consciousness. What if this consciousness is your real self? If this is the case, your true being is not limited to your physical body and consequently, you are not limited by death either. You *are*, beyond body, death and time.

Consciousness is the One supreme subject. It is not separate from any objects, animate or inanimate. It pervades and knows all that is, while remaining free from all that is.

Within each individual, consciousness is felt as inner Presence. It is what allows you to feel and know (thoughts and objects). Imagine looking at the ocean. All is vast and open. Within you, consciousness is this space of openness. When you look at life with conscious eyes, your mind is open and embraces reality as it is.

Introspection

You can also come to understand your true nature through introspection. The great Indian sage Ramana Maharshi used Self-enquiry, "Who am I?", as his method of introspection. [5] Paradoxically, when you cannot answer the question, you find the answer. What happens when you cannot find the answer to a question? Close your eyes and observe your mind. When you do not find any answers to a question, how is your mind? Your mind is blank, empty of any content. Still, there is something that recognises and knows this emptiness. This is Pure Consciousness, your true nature. It is you as Presence, neutral and open. Self-enquiry allows you to understand who you are, by directly accessing the Source of your being. From there, you are aware of all that comes and goes (objects, thoughts, feelings and inner states).

Now, feel *the watcher (or Father) quality* of Pure Consciousness. Observe how He watches, effortlessly, and how He knows, directly. He simply watches like a child does. Does the watcher judge? Does the watcher have ambitions, plans and

---

[5] *Be As You Are. The Teachings of Sri Ramana Maharshi*, edited by D.Godman, Penguin books, 1992.

14

programmes? The watcher is completely open, calm and neutral. Pure Consciousness glides over everything like a duck on a peaceful lake. This watcher is yourself in the most intimate and natural way. He is deeply yourself and hence it is not limited to "you". Pure Consciousness is One with all things - pure knowledge, pure intelligence.

Feel also *the heart (or Mother) quality* of Pure Consciousness. In this case, Pure Consciousness is like an open flower which vibrates in unison with all things. Feel how alive She is. Pure Consciousness has millions of hands to help you, all the forms to protect you and various faces to smile at you. She calls you through many people. She knows all the wisdom and all the mistakes of the world. She knows every being directly, absolutely. She knows what you need to grow and how to bring it to you. Because Pure Consciousness is One with everything, Pure Consciousness has only one will: love. Your true being is pure love.

However, despite this absolute intelligence and love, your true nature cannot always help you. Your mind has to be open enough to feel the presence of the Heart in the depth of yourself. Listen to its voice. It is also your inner voice, what feels the most natural in you. This Heart is You. Pure Consciousness is not mere emptiness or silence. It is the living presence of the Heart.

The Heart, love, is the key to the wonders of this world. It is the silent force flowing through all things. When your mind is open, you are One with the entire universe. This is why existence can speak to you, answer your questions and hold your hand. You are not separate from anything. You need only open your mind and let your heart guide you because it penetrates and knows all things.

Pure consciousness knows the Truth of all things: past, present and future. This knowledge can be grasped by the mind. This corresponds to a state of super-consciousness. It is the state of the Buddha with open eyes. Pure Consciousness can also manifest through you spontaneously, without the mind having the intellectual knowledge of it. This is the state of innocence. Innocence is equally beautiful because it crosses all shadows (the ego) without being affected. This is the state of the Buddha with closed eyes. Truth is known directly in the Heart.

Visual Examples

Finally, you can understand your true nature through visual examples. This was the easiest way for me. When you come to understanding this way, it is not intellectual. Suddenly, from deep within, you know. This understanding can no longer be questioned. Imagine the ocean. The waves come and go. They seem to be born and to die. Each wave appears distinct from the others. However, they all come from the same ocean (the same Source). They are not separate from one another. In reality, they have neither beginning nor end. They are all made from the same substance: the water, which made the waves of the past, shapes the present ones and will give rise to the waves of tomorrow. Whatever its form is, this water remains unchanged. Beyond appearances and time, in spite of the waves which come and go, nothing has ever fundamentally changed. Separation, as well as time, is nothing but a way the mind perceives reality. Despite the movement of the waves which come and go, the ocean *is*. It has always been and it will always be. Everything *is*, or more exactly, only Pure Consciousness *is*.

Like the waves in the ocean, individuals form one single being. If you identify yourself with a wave (with your body), you become afraid and you believe that when you reach the shore, your existence ends. But the wave which reaches the shore melts again into the ocean before taking form again and reaching the shore once more. This is the eternal dance of life. Like a wave, your spirit changes in form and returns to the ocean. This ocean knows everything because it is everything. Because it knows, it is called consciousness. You are Consciousness. When a wave ceases to consider itself as a simple wave and opens itself to its oceanic nature, it "returns" consciously to that place it has never left. This opening is liberation. You know your true nature as "I am".

For some other people, in particular children, it may be easier for them to understand their true nature while looking at a tree. Imagine that each branch of the tree ends with different aspects of Creation: human beings from all nationalities, animals, plants, stars. We all belong to the same tree and the same sap (Pure Consciousness) flows through everything. Do not only identify with a branch (your body). Each one of us is the whole tree. Therefore, it is important to be at peace with every branch of our tree as they are all parts of our Being. Oneness is the source of diversity and diversity is only an appearance in the realm of oneness.

Consciousness and Harmony

As long as you are not aware, your life is generally governed by "fears and selfish desires" (ego). Ego is a sort of programme registered in the memory of your cells. Depending on the branch of the tree you belong to, this programme is more or less loaded and influences your life. However, this programme is not truly you. When you really understand this, you can detach from your ego and be aware of it. Awareness is like the light that dispels darkness. Directly experience this. When you are conscious of your ego (e.g. you realise that you have been insensitive), insensitivity disappears. Being conscious brings harmony.

Of course, fears and selfish desires also have their use in the vast plan of the universe. Every difficulty is an opportunity to awake. This whole universe is about awakening and love. It is not about letting the ego act freely. How do I know this? Dive deeply within you to know the answer. When you listen to your heart, you also listen to the Heart of the universe. Each tentacle has the same "head". There is no separation. Answers are self-evident.

The Heart looks for balance and harmony. Observe how this universe functions. Everything takes place according to an order of equilibrium. This is the yin and the yang, the positive and negative

17

poles of universal energy. One cannot exist without the other: attraction without repulsion, abundance without lack, success without failure. Everything is interdependent. Thereby, like a see-saw, individuals alternate between highs and lows until they find the point of balance: the Heart.

As long as you do not find this point of balance, you reap what you sow. Judging others unfairly is judging your own self and lacking respect for others is not respecting who you are. Of course, this also goes the other way around: caring for others is caring for your own self and respecting your inner voice is another way of respecting others. This is the "boomerang effect" of life. In this way, life teaches you how to behave, until you find your own inner guide: the Heart. Yet, this "boomerang effect" does not explain everything about the functioning of life. When people have problems or experience difficulties, it does not always mean that they "deserve" them! Some negative events are not produced by karma.[6] Therefore, it is important to refrain from hasty judgment. For example, avoid saying to the people who experience a difficult situation that this happens to them because they have a problem. "The Heart has reasons that the reason cannot know". Life is more profound and mysterious than all logical deductions. If you have the tendency to judge and criticise, observe how sages behave. Have you ever seen the sculpture of the wise monkeys? They close their eyes, ears and mouths. They take distance from perception (from what they see, hear and think). Relationships are much more easy-going and enjoyable when hasty judgments and conclusions do not cloud people's minds.

---

[6] The law of "cause and effect". Consequences of previous actions.

Consciousness and Existence

Everything is part of consciousness: all beings, animals, plants, clouds, stars and also time. The past is eternally present. "Here and now" includes the totality of existence. It is the sap that nourishes the whole tree. According to the scientist J. Bousquet, oneness can be explained because "shapes are informed and informative."[7] He also describes how past information can be incorporated into the present through light (electromagnetic waves). This accounts for the fact that every form is the result of a pre-existing knowledge. Creation is the result of Pure Consciousness. It is like a flower unfolding from the seed.

Everything is in everything. The spirit of everything is at the core of each cell.[8] The whole universe is within you. Through the heart, you are One with existence, beyond time. This is the reason why you can, for example, keep contact with beloved ones who have

---

[7] In a scientific paper on the *Transfer of Information in Living Organisms*, J. Bousquet wrote: "Our hypothesis is that shapes are informed and informative. This is due to a wave (a vibration) which determines the corresponding shape. All shapes are the result of a conscious knowledge (from the past) that decodes its future content from its own structure, like the butterfly is already coded in the caterpillar or the oak tree in the acorn." Webmaster555.free.fr.

[8] The physicist Jean E. Charon explained that "Some elementary particles, the electrons, are steady particles (their life span is quasi infinite). They constitute mineral, vegetal and human organisms". He showed that these particles contain within a sort of shield, a new space-time. He compares this to "Soap bubbles that would float within our ordinary space-time. Within these tiny bubbles, there exists a special space-time that is closed to the outside. Our ordinary space-time, the one of matter, goes from past to future and energy decreases over time. Matter is bound to die. In the space-time of the bubbles, it is a cyclic time. Past events are continuously brought back into the present. Information is never lost and keeps increasing. It is a structure that learns from experience. Isn't this dimension the one of the Spirit?" Jean E. Charon, *L'Esprit cet inconnu*, Albin Michel, 1978.

left their bodies. Separation does not exist. Because separation does not exist, the spirit of the sages is also at the core of each individual. Talk to them. Pray to them. They "hear" you. Similarly, when you hear your inner voice, you hear the voice of your spiritual Mothers and Fathers. This Heart calls you, cares for you and protects you. This Heart is all around you and it is also You. You simply need to open your mind. You have always been One with the Heart and the universe.

Pure Consciousness is always One with all that *is*. This is why the Heart holds everything. Stillness is the source of movement. "Nothing" is the reason for everything. Emptiness supports the whole. Pure Consciousness and existence are intimately entwined. They form a single whole Being. They are like the two sides of the same coin. It is an eternal love story. The manifested world is not an absolute illusion.[9] The only true illusion is strictly identifying with the body and believing in separation. Pure Consciousness is within every form. Forms play their role in the vast theatre of consciousness. How could Pure Consciousness know itself without Creation? Consciousness and existence are interdependent and One.

Consciousness is One but consciousness has different forms. Consequently, it has, on the surface, more or less clarity about itself. It is like a lamp. Its centre is very luminous (the Heart) and the outside is darker (the shape, ego). The clear aspect of consciousness (commonly called Truth, Pure Consciousness, the Source, the Self or the Heart) is the watcher who can differentiate what is true from what is false. Truth includes non-truth. Non-duality includes duality. Pure Consciousness includes unconsciousness. Because consciousness has different aspects, consciousness plays hide and seek with itself. In this way, you can also say that consciousness is unconsciousness. But what sense does this make? You can also distinguish true

---

[9] According to the philosophy "Advaita Saiva" of Kashmir, "The universe is perfectly real. Given that Shakti, the Divine energy is real, that which emanates from this energy is also real". Jaideva Singh, *The Secret of Self-Recognition,* Motilal Banarsidass publishers private limited, Delhi, p.23.

Consciousness from ego consciousness. You can examine it from different angles. This is why it is better not to define it too much, intellectually. You could get lost in definitions and concepts. Intellectual definitions are limited. Feel the truth in your heart.

Truth is very simple. What does your heart tell you? What does your heart feel as Truth? Can you recognise truth when it echoes in you? Be silent to understand the real meaning of love, sensitivity, "nothingness", "emptiness" and non-duality. Dive deeply within yourself to go beyond concepts and words, and even beyond the rejection of concepts and words. Allow also the dream *to be* because Creation is the most beautiful dream. Embrace all that *is*, because Pure Consciousness and ego consciousness are part of the same oneness. Pure Consciousness is within each cell and every form. This is why your inner self has clarity about the outer reality. But the ego and the outside world are often ignorant of the inner light. Reality can be bright inside and outside. This is *conscious oneness*. Conscious oneness is the destination of this universe. It is also the real beginning of life, in a universe where the usual space-time is no longer the reference because life *is*, beyond time. In the infinite thread of time, the flower of Creation will reach its full bloom.

Consciousness and Perfection

The universe is based on a principle of equilibrium. Whatever individuals do, everything returns to balance.[10] This is the play of energies, the divine game of existence. Everything is absolutely perfect. Even when the world goes topsy-turvy, it does so in a perfect

---

[10] For the scientists, "The world is governed by laws of physics which provide equilibrium to our environment. *Each and every element plays an important role and regulates itself automatically in symbiosis with the other elements.* We can consider this world as a collection of agents who dialogue between themselves in order to obtain *a personal and global stability*". Fabien Vauchelles, *Algorithms from Nature* (information on the web).

21

manner. Whatever people fear or desire, it generates the most optimal conditions to awaken their minds. Even imperfections are perfect. Everything, including the lack of awareness, leads to Self-realisation.

When you are not aware, you believe that you are free to do and create whatever you want. Yet, you are only the puppet of your mental conditioning and of the divine play. All that which happens to you is predictable. You are never totally free, in the egoic sense of freedom: "I can do whatever I want". You are either under the control of the ego (fears and selfish desires) or under the guidance of the Heart. Paradoxically, by giving up your personal will and listening to your heart, you find the freedom to really be yourself and to create. *To create does not mean that you can manifest all that you wish.* The real Creator has no personal will. Creation simply happens. When it is clear that you are not your body but the essence that includes all bodies, selfish desires are meaningless. The divine play leads you to understand this.

Selfishness cannot really make you happy and peaceful. If you want to be the driver of your vehicle (you want to work in a specific field, you desire a certain type of partner, you wish for a certain amount of money, salary or success), you risk making detours through your life path before reaching the final destination. However, every detour is useful to awake and return to the Heart. But it is still preferable to take a seat behind your vehicle and let the Heart drive you.

The Heart is a very experienced driver who knows every aspect of you and of the universe. Pure Consciousness is within every form. So let yourself be carried. Surrender. Let go of your desire to control your life. For example, if your ego wants to do a specific job, there are good chances that you will meet some people who can help you fulfil your desire. It may seem that you are on the right path. Nonetheless, this reality is conditioned by your desires. It does not necessarily correspond to your natural potential.[11] On the other hand, when your

---

[11] Consciousness is in every cell of the body and knows the individual body/mind potential. Naturally, when ego is passive, Consciousness directly manifests this potential.

mind is open like space and ego does not influence you, your true nature is completely free to express itself through you. In which case, life guides you. External phenomena are the manifestations of the inner truth. For example, you see ten advertisements for the same job in one day or you meet someone whose job really inspires you. A natural movement takes place. Life clearly shows you the direction.

One night, I had a funny dream. In nature, there were electric tracks and upon these tracks ran supermarket trolleys. Some people could not let go of the idea they were not in control of the trolleys. They were holding on to them firmly. Other people though, were sitting contentedly inside the trolleys and letting themselves be carried. Why not relax and cease to worry? When you follow the inner flow (the Heart), you are upon electric tracks. You are taken care of by existence itself. Simply connect to the Heart. When the Heart is the guide, it directly reaches inner peace and harmony. You can relax, let yourself be carried and even sleep on the natural tracks. On the other hand, you need to quickly awake if ego leads you because it goes against the flow. You go against the natural flow of life each time fears and selfish desires influence you. So leave behind your fears and expectations. Follow your inner voice. And if sometimes you have to lose, accept losing since it is surely in order to win in a deeper sense. In truth, there are no losers in the "game" of life.

Consciousness and Heart

Pure Consciousness is at the core of everything and is all inclusive. This is why Pure Consciousness is the Heart. The Heart freely expresses itself when ego does not interfere. So let go of your personal will. Surrender. This is the state of "non-doing" Taoism speaks about. Actually, this is the "non-doing" of ego only. Without ego interfering, your true nature can directly act through you. Non-doing should not be understood as passivity.

23

Besides, surrendering to the Heart does not mean following any stream of life. If you say "yes" to all invitations on your way, you may not be able to achieve what you really wanted to do during the day. The leaf swirls in the air. It has no goal and no direction. It goes where the wind blows. Is this really surrendering to the flow of life? Awareness is the direction. When you know that everything is One, harmony is the natural choice. This requires sometimes the ability to say "no" to certain currents of life if they are not flowing towards balance and harmony. Real surrender is when harmony (for yourself and others) influences your choices and decisions. For example, you enjoy having a drink with your friends in a pub, but you also know when it is time to leave in order to take care of your family, your work or yourself. In this case, you are mature enough not to be influenced by your ego or the ego of other people.

Being spiritual simply means listening to the Heart. Our destination is love and harmony. When you listen to your heart, decisions are not influenced by the outside world. *They come from a spontaneous inner movement.* Simply, it feels natural to say or do such and such things (e.g. to accept or refuse a situation, to be active or to do nothing). When you are sensitive to general harmony (for you and others), as well as detached from people's opinions, your heart expresses itself freely. For instance, if the decision not to work is harmonious in your life and does not disturb the life of the people around you, then no matter what people may think, you know it is the right decision for you.

The water from the river is in flow and the water from the lake remains still. By listening to your inner voice, you know what is natural for you. Do not compare your life with that of others. We all live what we need to live. The natural order is perfect. We should learn from it. Nature also shows us that the flow of the river goes over the pebbles but goes around the larger rocks. By listening to your inner voice, you know the best way to preserve harmony. For example, you can accept reality as it is without suffering the burden of it. You do not have to overcome all difficulties. You can bypass the main obstacles. Listen to your inner voice.

Following your inner voice (and not your personal will) is not the absence of individual participation. I once heard a story about a man sitting on top of his house while the water was rising due to heavy rain. He asked God for help and a helicopter came. But the man was expecting something more extraordinary from God: "God can stop the rain". So he did not wave at the helicopter to get help. He kept on waiting and praying. God sent a second and a third helicopter. The third time he could not refuse His help. Divine help is also brought simply by the people who surround you. God's hands are also people's hands. Divine help is not always extraordinary. It is your responsibility to recognise it and act accordingly.

When there is true surrender, spontaneity, naturalness and pure actions unfold without the interference of the mind. In fact, just be very natural in all circumstances and while facing your indecisions, ask yourself the following question: "What is the simplest, most natural, self-evident and harmonious solution?" Of course, you cannot always be clear about what decision to make. How do you surrender your personal will to the Heart and do what is really natural? When you have doubts, trust life to direct you in the clearest way. A few more hints can also help you gain clarity:

> *Surrender to harmony.* Be sensitive to others and to your own feelings. For example, you can feel an uneasy inner sensation when you have selfish intentions. If so, do not listen to your mind which may try to seduce you by saying: "Just be free. Why do you care about that?" Conscious freedom, unity and harmony directly lead to the Heart. Selfish freedom and division move away from It. Choices are clear.

> *Surrender to trust.* Do not let fears lead you. If the climbing plant hides the sun, the gardener intervenes to let the light shine. There is always help on the road. Do not doubt the Divine's presence and intelligence. Miracles can also happen when they are really needed. Be trusting.

Surrender to your limitations. Remain vigilant. The tree is flexible. It moves in the wind. But flexibility also has limits. Be aware of your own limitations and act accordingly. Self-respect is as important as your respect for others.

Surrender to divine intelligence. Wish for Light only in order to have clarity or solve a problem. Do not wish for anything personal (money, success or romantic love). The creative force of the Light is then free to manifest in the most harmonious and optimal way to bring you just what you need (not always what your ego would like) and to solve your problem.

Surrender to being patient. Do not rush into easy solutions. Sometimes, patience is the only answer. Know how to relax. When the time is ripe, you know what to do without any doubts. Wait for clarity to come.

To understand your true nature is a great help in living your daily life freely.

Chapter 3: Understanding the Mind

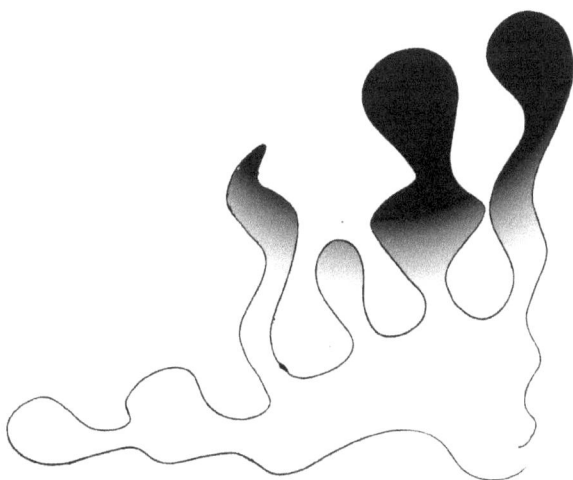

What is Ego?

As human beings, we have sophisticated brains which allow us to think. We develop mental intelligence. Mental intelligence is both useful and deceitful. It is useful because it is an analytical and intelligent tool (without which we couldn't actually open to Universal Consciousness). It brings our understanding of reality into question. On the other hand, mental intelligence is deceitful. As soon as individuals identify with their body, thoughts and emotions, they position themselves as different and apart from one another, like the tentacles who believed they were different from the octopus. This belief generates the feeling of separation and consequently, judgments, taboos, guilt, fears and selfish desires. This leads to suffering, the fear of Truth, and unconsciousness. One's true identity is forgotten. Unconsciousness enters the realm of Pure Consciousness (non-duality).

Ego is Pure Consciousness limited by false beliefs. Hence, at the core of limited consciousness is unlimited consciousness. The Heart is ever present. To illustrate this, we can take the metaphor of boiling water. When water boils, it takes different shapes and makes bubbles. Each bubble is like a contraction of water. Yet, it is still water. Similarly, ego is the contraction of Pure Consciousness. Yet, it is still Pure Consciousness. In this sense, mind and no-mind are the same. Only false beliefs prevent individual consciousness from realising it *is* Universal Consciousness, One with all that is. Each tentacle is One with the octopus.

Pure Consciousness is the Light that distinguishes the truth from the illusion (ego). Yet, Pure Consciousness does not reject the ego. There is no duality. It simply knows - through the mind that is conscious and/or through the sensitivity of the heart that is awakened. Hence, you know what is fair and what is not. You know what brings true love and joy and what does not. Given the fact that Pure Consciousness knows, it makes choices. Pure Consciousness has a direction. All the planets orbit the sun in the same direction. Your true nature knows what creates balance and harmony. Consequently, if your "room" is still dark, understanding your true nature and the ego, will allow you to find the Light and to listen to your heart. Your life has a meaning and a direction.

Ego and False Beliefs

The ego-mind is conditioned. The natural mind is spontaneous. In general, depending on circumstances, you either operate from the ego-mind or the natural mind. Why then does ego influence you sometimes? From birth, your mind has been shaped by many subjective experiences and definitions. This has resulted in a pool of labels and a sense of "I". These labels give an idea of what you are and what the world is: "I am like this", "She is like that" and "The world is such and such". These labels are never neutral. They are all coloured by personal experiences. Personal experiences shape your opinions and influence your actions. If you have been disturbed by certain words or behaviour, it is likely that you experience life through a personal filter. This filter distorts your perception of reality. For example, if a friend forgets to say "Hello", you may think it is intentional.

When you understand that your mind is influenced by subjective perceptions, you can question the way you perceive reality: "Am I right?" Some people never question their perception. They first tend to believe they are right and others are wrong. This type of behaviour is often the result of deep hidden fears. These fears generate strong self-defence mechanisms. Is this the case for you? On the other hand, some people question themselves too much and tend to think their own views are wrong and others are right. Often, this hides another deep "wound": guilt. Guilt can create excessive self-judgment and excessive tolerance of disrespectful behaviour. Do you belong to this category?

Whatever "wound" you have, it is clear that it makes you see reality in a distorted way. Therefore, keep in mind that your perception of people and events may be wrong. With this understanding, you can watch your mental movie without being lost in it. Mind does not have to disappear. The sky has clouds. Mental concepts, beliefs, "I" thoughts should not be condemned. They are what they are. Simply, do not take them too seriously. You think someone is distant. Is this really the case? You believe this other one is extravagant. Is it really true? You know someone is not good. Are you so sure about it? You are sure of your opinion. Can you remain open to other people's opinions? You are certain that your way of doing things is the best. Can you consider other methods? Actually, by simply taking distance from your perceptions and so called "certitudes", mind disappears. Yet, do not look for the disappearance of the mind. Be conscious of its content. This is enough to set you free from the ego. When you are conscious, the watcher is present. Pure Consciousness is the Presence that tells the mind: "This is ego. Do not pay attention to it. Let go". Consciousness is freedom.

Ego and Judgments

I shall tell you a little story. Every day, a man sat by the shore of a lake. He would look for hours at its serene waters. Behind him, a little road led to a village. One day, a drunken man happened to pass by. Looking at the man by the lake, he thought he was also drunk and had to rest before going on. He laughed into his beard and tottered again on the road. A few hours later a sad man walked by. Seeing this man alone by the lake, he believed he was also sad. At that moment, the man of the lake moved and a knife fell from his pocket. "Could he also be dangerous?" the sad man thought, while quickly moving away. Later on came a jealous lady, an angry boy, a happy woman and a fearful man. All of them projected different faces onto the man by the lake. They were actually looking at their own reflection. Only a child, who happened to be there, saw the peacefulness of both the lake and the man alike. They were One.

Only innocent eyes see the truth. On the other hand, there are misconceptions about others when perception is veiled by ego. Most of the time, opinions are based on objective facts, but these facts may be amplified or distorted to the extent of imagining a totally new reality. These are the projections of the ego-mind. Whenever ego influences you, you do not see others as they are but as you think they are. Therefore, you hold onto all the signs that seem to confirm your views. You find so-called "proof" or arguments to justify your beliefs. This is how the ego deceives itself and can be a merciless judge. This is especially the case when you think you belong to the "good side", whenever you are sure of your values and certain to be right or "politically/spiritually correct". Being on the "good" side can be an excuse to justify your beliefs and lack of openness. Ego can then appear as non-ego. Appearances are misleading.

What is defined as correct also determines what is meant by incorrect. This may lead people to be judgmental. Before the sensitivity of your heart is awakened, it is useful to have points of reference concerning appropriate behaviour. However, it is equally important to understand that it is all relative. Natural behaviour cannot be limited to specific rules. It depends upon circumstances. In some cases, a little bit of conditioning is necessary (natural fertilisers help the plants grow better). Raising the voice can be useful at times (the atmosphere is clearer after the storm). So refrain from judging (even judgments!). There cannot be any strict definitions about what proper natural behaviour is.

Would it not be detrimental to make judgments or criticisms a taboo? *Freedom of expression is fundamental.* As long as free expression is conscious (e.g. you do not gossip or try to hurt anyone), feel free to have a critical mind, to express your views or to confide freely in a friend in order to get something off your mind. Express what you feel. Call a spade a spade. But do not take your opinion too seriously! You may be wrong, or a situation you do not agree with may change in the future. Be aware, though, of the quality of your judgments. There is a difference between closed judgments and open judgments. If you are able to express your disagreement freely while remaining open to other views, this is highly beneficial to everybody. This is the way we grow. This is how we evolve. The outcome is often a more open view and it gives room for clarification. When people look at the countryside through a window, one person sees the fruit tree, another one the squirrel on the branch, the flowers in the garden or the thorny bush. Perceptions are subjective. Individual consciousness is generally limited. Knowing this, you can keep in mind that you may be wrong. This incertitude is a part of freedom for your own self and others. Yet, do not undermine your opinion by saying "It is all relative". Some perceptions are true. Concepts and opinions are useful. For example, the definition of a clean house varies from one individual to the other. This does not mean that you cannot define what is clean. There is common sense in all of us. This common sense reflects the general agreement on the meaning of "cleanliness". This common sense is also the intuitive knowledge of the inner truth (Pure Consciousness - our ancestral wisdom). In this way, you can distinguish what is true from what is false and you can remain coherent, personally and socially. Points of reference are necessary. If some people call a peacock the blue bird and others the green bird, we will no longer understand what bird we are talking about. Concepts and definitions are obviously useful to provide clarity. To free yourself from the mind does not mean no longer using it. You can use your mind as a useful tool while remaining the master of it.

Ego and Guilt

When people identify with ego, they may feel ashamed of their thoughts and behaviour. They may feel guilt; but who is responsible? As long as you are not aware, you are not responsible. Your "wound" is responsible. Do not identify with it. It is only false beliefs. The root of these beliefs is often very old. The past is the past. Leave it behind. It is useless to point fingers at people. It is also useless to identify yourself with the victim or the guilty. If you feel guilty, let go of all these limited identifications. Simply understand your "wound": the ego. Ego is within you but you are not truly the ego. Ego is a "programme" in your cells. It is a temporary movie only. The fact of understanding who you truly are (the screen and not the film), sets you free from ego identification and guilt. Does this allow a total freedom?

Some people say: "I am not the doer therefore I am not responsible. There is nothing I can do". Besides, ego plays its role on the stage of consciousness. So, you can legitimately wonder why you should try to prevent its influence. Indeed, ego is a programme within you and you are not responsible for it. Therefore, you should not feel "bad" or guilty. Yet, this understanding should not be an excuse to surrender to ego! The play is all about being conscious. Remember who you are. Every tentacle is the octopus. Everything is You. When you are conscious and understand who you really are and what ego is, detachment happens and your behaviour changes. You can watch your ego without identifying with it. Naturally, it loses its influence. For example, you can admit that your ego has annoyed your neighbour and consequently, you do your best to improve the situation. Who is now the doer?

Without ego your mind is not active. You do not calculate and you do not have any fixed plans. This may be felt as strange or disturbing. You may feel a sort of void or emptiness within you. You may also be afraid of losing control. Who is the doer when thinking stops? The sunflower does not have a mind but it naturally turns to the sun. Similarly, without ego, a natural movement takes place. Without mind, there is *pure knowledge* and *pure action.* You do not think but thoughts arise in your mind. You do not have a plan but the plan clearly appears. You do not act but actions manifest. For example, the solution to the problem with your neighbour suddenly pops up in your mind. And when no solution comes, what should you do? There is nothing wrong with having no clarity. This simply means that the time for clarity and action has not yet come. Relax. Wait. There always comes a time when the decision to make is self-evident, choices are clear and a movement takes place within you, or outside. Who is the doer then? It is Pure Consciousness, the Heart. Who are you truly? Do you still see a difference between You and the Heart?

For some people, "I" means the Heart and for others the ego. Depending on the meaning of "I", you can say "I am the doer" or "I am not the doer". Every point of view is right when there is clarity about definitions. But let us not play with words and angles of perception. This could create confusion. Most of the time, it is only an egoic intellectual game. When you see that you are trapped in this game, do not judge your mind and feel guilty. Simply return to the Heart and inner silence.

Ego and Fears

Ego also contains the programme "irrational fears". Irrational fears have no reason to exist in the present moment. They are pure illusions. However, when your mind is in control, irrational fears may appear. Simply understand who you truly are. By finding the Source of your Being, irrational fears vanish.

Observe your fears like clouds in the sky, with detachment. What happens then? They dissolve. Your mind is again like the space: open, empty, totally peaceful and satisfied. This is truly you and it can never be taken away from you. Observe this in daily life. Each time fears, selfish desires and hasty judgments appear in your mind, be conscious of them. Do not get carried away by them. By returning to the Source (the open and neutral Presence), ego dissolves. Your mind is like an elastic cord attached to a fixed point. The cord moves and stretches out until the movement stops and the cord returns to stillness. Ego appears and disappears but your true nature is permanent. Your Presence (the fixed point) is always there. Even when you get carried away by your mental movie, there is still something in you that can recognise the movie, is it not true? Consciousness is always present. There is no reason to be afraid. Believe in yourself and existence.

Ego and Desires

When you believe that you have lost contact with your true nature, which is already completely satisfied, you search for satisfaction outside. Hence, by lack of understanding, ego wants "more and more and better and better". Ego has desires, expectations and consequently dissatisfaction. When ego is strong, satisfaction is rare. Ego generally pushes, anticipates, compares and is afraid of not getting the best of all life possibilities.

As far as children's education is concerned, the mind has the tendency to favour social success over personal development. The opposite is also true. In such cases, children are requested to learn many things in many fields. This may induce situations where the mind is saturated with too much knowledge and cannot be connected with its true inner intelligence. This may also induce situations where there are too many activities, knowledge is scattered and learning is superficial. Reacting against this phenomenon and "doing nothing" is not the solution either.

Personal flowering and social success are not contradictory - both can be achieved. Is the solution not the middle way? If so, there is a time for everything. There is a time for originality, creativity and a time for steady, simple and methodical academic learning. There is a time for free play and expression and a time for discipline and concentration. There is a time for the body and there is a time for the intellect. There is a time for being with others and a time for inner silence. In any case, when children are respected, they are naturally in tune with their inner silence. Their inner intelligence guides them. This allows personal and social harmony. The seeds contain the flowers to come. By giving the best of ourselves and all the warmth of our love, the seeds become beautiful flowers. "Education is the development of the whole being. Head, Heart and Hand – all three must be trained by artistic, scientific and practical education. The body, mind, intellect and spirit must have harmonious development."[12]

Mental Behaviour and Natural Behaviour

In the following paragraphs, I describe several types of behaviour in order to clearly distinguish natural behaviour from mental behaviour. For example, when you operate from the ego-mind, you tend to behave systematically. You may decide to never give money to beggars because you think it is useless. Or, on the contrary, you may decide to always give them something if you believe it is useful. Natural behaviour is not systematic. Depending on the present moment and circumstances, you feel whether to give beggars some money or not. The less you think, the less you calculate and the more you allow life to flow and reveal its wonders. The beggar to whom you gave your money can very well spend it in a pub and meet a person who changes his life.

People open to the flow of life may seem irrational. They behavior does not always appear logical. Actually, being sensitive to the present moment is the only true and meaningful direction. Of course, this may induce a more unforeseeable and unsteady life. Actions do not happen according to an agenda. And if there is an agenda, the mind is still open to changes. For example, a family may plan to go somewhere during the holidays, but if they suddenly feel it is better to stay at home, they will stay at home despite all their planning.

What influences natural behaviour? Is it not the sense of well-being, balance and harmony? In general, natural people do not force themselves to accept out of interest, fear or guilt situations they do not

---

[12] Purnima Zweers, *Spiritual Education,* "Swami Sivananda on education", Indica Books, Varanasi, p.33.

like. They simply follow what feels right from within. They have intuition. Often, I notice that there is an idealistic understanding of what is meant by being spiritual. The myth is that a spiritual person is absolutely calm, silent and never angry. However, without ego, you are simply natural. Depending on circumstances, you may even be very talkative, excited or angry. When you are natural, you are spontaneous. You let your true nature express itself freely. You go with its flow. Let us be clear about this expression. Going with the flow does not mean that you have to accept any type of situation in daily life. For example, when a situation is unfair, do not be submissive. Naturally express your disagreement or do your best so that justice is done. The inner "yes" is not an obstacle to the outer "no". Self-respect is as important as the respect for others. Only thus can you remain open to the Heart and follow its flow. Natural boundaries can be set. These boundaries come from the Heart understanding. They are not the result of rejection, a desire to hurt or a feeling of revenge. Natural boundaries preserve harmony. For example, for the sake of general harmony, you restrict access to your working place. Your inner voice knows what the harmonious balance is. Follow the flow of your heart.

When you operate from the ego-mind, you cannot understand intuitive behaviour. Intuitive behaviour seems risky or immature. It does not follow logic and conventions. It does not take into account lessons from the past either. The idea of risk only makes sense to the ego-mind. Risk is not relevant to the natural mind. Listening to the inner voice counts first. For example, opening a shop in a nice place (but not too far from the commercial centre), feels like a better idea than opening it in the most commercial street. We are all different. By listening to our inner nature, we naturally find our place. We are in harmony with the environment and the different elements around.

When you are in tune with your inner rhythm, you are also in harmony with the natural order. For example, while walking slowly on a path, you do not even crush the little ant and the snake has the time to escape. However, harmony is not only the result of slow or calm behaviour. Let us take as an example the traffic in India. How can there be so few accidents? Cows, children, pedestrians, cars, bicycles, motorbikes, dogs, everything and everybody is in the street! It seems to be total chaos. However, there is a perfect order amongst this chaos. People find their place and slip into the traffic as if by magic. In general, no one thinks. Everybody goes into the traffic without fear and in this way, there is harmony. Not thinking widens the field of possibilities. This is difficult to believe because the general conditioning is that without thinking or planning you put yourself at risk. The opposite, however, is true.

Given the fact that for every truth there is a counter-truth, I have reservations about not thinking. When mental habits and fears are strong, not thinking can be more detrimental than beneficial. If your true nature is suppressed because of fears, it cannot express itself freely and be in command. Your mind is in control. Accept this. Do not force anything. Just watch your fears without judging them. Progressively, they disappear. On the other hand, when your true nature is not limited by fears, it is completely free to be in command. When ego does not interfere, the Heart spontaneously guides you. Your true nature is One with all that is and, therefore, it "knows" and spontaneously feels how to act or deal with situations. Deep within, there is a sensitivity, a wisdom, a discernment of an unbelievable force and intelligence. You can totally trust this force and surrender to it. But how can you really surrender? How can you listen to your heart? When an empty bottle is closed with a cork, nature's fresh air cannot enter into the bottle. How can you remove the cork (the ego)? How can the inside and the outside unite and be what they have always been: the same air flowing through all things?

Chapter 4: Opening to the Heart

Marie, 7 years old.

Heart and States of Consciousness

Tell me friend,
Is there time to rest?
Is there time to listen to yourself?
Do you let "wounds" confess?

It is time.
Nourish yourself, listen to yourself.
Taking time for yourself
Is not wasting time.
Simply see who you are and fully express
The Child inside you,
Calling you, endlessly.

Your inner child never stops calling you but as long as your mind is closed, you cannot hear the call. On the other hand, when your mind opens because it no longer rejects itself, then all the veils are removed from the face of love.

To open to the Heart, the great Indian sage Ramana Maharshi advocated "tracing the 'I'-thought (ego) back to its source and maintaining awareness of the 'I'-thought until it dissolves in the source from which it came."[13] This technique is called Self-enquiry and Ramana Maharshi "constantly recommended it as the most direct and efficient way of discovering the unreality of the "I" thought". Let us take as an example the thought "I don't love myself". Some of us believe in this thought, although it is only a false idea, a conditioning. If you observe this thought and the corresponding emotion, you see that who you are is neither the thought nor the emotion but the watcher of them. In this sense, ego is an illusion. With awareness, thoughts and emotions dissolve. Yet, is it easy to be aware of ego in

---

[13] *Be As You Are. The Teachings of Sri Ramana Maharshi,* ibid., pp.46-47.

daily life? Can the mind return to its Source (the Heart) effortlessly? Let us see how individual consciousness operates in general.

The Mental State

In the mental state, Pure Consciousness is, on the surface, limited by ego. The mind believes in false ideas, such as "I am not happy" or "She does not like me". When beliefs are strong, it is not possible to question them and to take distance from them. Ego influences your behaviour. For example, the thought "I am not happy" may result in the decision "I won't go out tonight". The thought "She does not like me" may provoke the reaction "I will ignore her". The root of ego is the belief "I am not good". Consequently, it is very important to understand how false this belief is. Ego is not who you truly are. This understanding is the basis for self-healing and inner peace.

Although "I" thoughts are not true, they still exist in most minds. Consequently, they may have effects in life. For example, false ideas may lead to wrong accusations. Whenever you identify with ego, you cannot face the consequences of your thoughts and behaviour. You cannot be the neutral and detached observer of your ego. It is too disturbing. Guilt is too strong. At this stage, there is too much resistance for the practice of Self-enquiry in daily life. When ego disturbs the mind, the Source, although always present, cannot be found.

The State of Unsteady Awareness

In the state of unsteady awareness, the mind is aware of "I" thoughts and can detach from them. However, self-reconciliation is not deep enough so mental tendencies persist. For example, you can detach from the thought "She does not like me" but it soon reappears in the mind because the idea is still disturbing. As long as you cannot believe that you are truly "good", ego remains active. Self-enquiry is possible but maintaining a state of Presence may be difficult and strenuous in some situations.

The State of Steady Awareness

When you know ego is not who you truly are, you are not in conflict with it. The mind is steady and detached. Ego is part of the Self but the Self is not the ego. The cloud is in the sky but the sky is not the cloud. You can grasp "I" thoughts and detach from them more and more easily. For example, the thoughts "She does not like me" or "I am not good" arise in the mind but they are not taken seriously. Yet, faced with new situations, the ego may still disturb you. Old mental habits tend to reappear. But as you are aware, you can quickly rediscover your inner peace. In such cases, the practice of Self-enquiry is a precious help.

Ego may also be very subtle and refined. Then it is not easy to be aware of it. When individual consciousness identifies with the peaceful, spiritual or kind-hearted person, it may play this role and therefore, it may lack sincerity. The subtle ego remains almost unnoticed but still, it influences the behaviour. The subtle ego tries to prove its superiority. It is the most deceitful of all. However, the subtle ego loses its influence when you are aware of it and when you understand that everybody has a subtle ego. *Are you aware of your subtle ego? What does it want to prove?* When the subtle ego is recognised and accepted, self-reconciliation is deep. It is no longer necessary to pay attention to "I" thoughts. The Heart grasps them instantly in its own way.

The Natural State

The natural state is the consciousness of the Heart. When you are able to laugh about everything, including the imperfections within yourself, you rediscover your inner child and your innocence. This is the natural state. There is no resistance to the truth of what is "here and now". For example, you do not deny that there is a cloud in your sky. You are not trapped by any role.

Self-enquiry allows returning to inner silence by observing the content of the mind ("I" thoughts). However, this silence may still be somewhat "technical". It is the result of a method. It is not yet the fruit of a true inner reconciliation. This silence may be felt as a sort of "indifferent emptiness". The sensitivity of the heart is not yet completely awakened.

In the natural state, the mind does not need to observe its content. It is directly connected to the Heart. It "knows" spontaneously. The inner silence is felt as « spontaneous emptiness ». When the mind rests in the Heart, the individual is sensitive and feels situations (e.g. whether it is better to get fully involved in a situation or to take distance from it). The Heart is not indifferent. It favours as much as possible unity and harmony. People's interests are taken as much into account as personal interests. The Heart's consciousness awakens when you are reconciled with your ego. There is no resistance and no duality. The mind is peaceful and silent. In this silence, naturalness expresses itself. Therefore, the people who are naturally silent are generally spontaneous, open and joyful. Like children, they observe and welcome reality as it is: without judging it, without referring to the past and without ideas about the future. Children have no distance from reality (what is present "here and now"). They feel it always in their Heart. They are "One" with it. Hence, like a diamond, the Heart reflects the surrounding colours. The Heart is a mirror.

The Heart is light because it does not have anything to prove or any need to pretend. This is the reason why the Heart may not, in certain cases, correspond to people's expectations about love. Naturalness expresses itself freely. Pure Consciousness can also take a fiery form when the situation warrants it. It is better to avoid trying to understand the Heart through the mind. It cannot be known this way because the true self expresses itself differently according to circumstances and individuals. Sometimes, its expression can be surprising and unexpected. Pure Consciousness also manifests differently according to one's own nature. For example, it is natural for some people to be silent and for others to be talkative. It is natural for some to live in communities while others prefer to be isolated. Some like to be active and others enjoy stillness. Some are gentle and others mischievous. We are "One" but each "one" has its own fragrance. Pure Consciousness has many forms and names but still, it is the same One reality. Each branch of the tree contains the same sap.

Some people have never left the natural state. Their heart has always guided them. Yet, they have not completely understood what their true nature is. "Who are you truly?" Can you answer this question in your own words? Self-realisation can be direct and effortless for you. Open your eyes because your true nature already embraces all things. You recognise beauty and godliness in everybody and in everything. Your mind is at peace. Love is a natural spring which flows and expresses itself through you.

So, from the mental state to the natural state, Pure Consciousness expresses itself differently. To sum up, we can say that Pure Consciousness is either: *limited* by ego (on the surface), *unsteady* and wavering between ego and Heart, *steady* but still subtly influenced by ego, and *natural* when the mind is open to truth and rests in the Heart. Consciousness changes states (and forms) until it becomes aware of itself and realises its true nature. Then, there is no duality because even duality is integrated.

Therefore, as long as your mind is disturbed by ego, attention should be given to "I" thoughts. How can you be conscious of them? How can you be free from the ego's negative influence? Is it enough to say, as I hear sometimes, that "ego is an illusion" to free yourself from it? Can we deny the reality of the illusion? Intellectually, it is possible to assert: "I am not the ego". However, as long as there is identification with ego in daily life, you cannot deny its influence. Ego plays its role.

47

Opening to the Heart "Here and Now"

Individual consciousness can open to the Heart. In order to do this, the fear of truth has to be overcome. Generally, we tend to be afraid of truth because we do not want to see what ego has done to our Being: separation, judgment, rejection and guilt. Unconsciousness is the result of this. However, when the mind opens to truth and accepts the ego as it is, transformation happens without even looking for it. Metal transforms into gold (alchemy). For example, when you recognise that your beliefs are wrong (e.g. "This person is not good"), wrong beliefs disappear. Your mind is free and love can flow.

We all are at different stages of personal development, at different places on our paths of evolution. Some people are more advanced and wise. Others are still at the beginning of their path or somewhere in the middle. This is not important. What truly matters is not to reach a different place but to completely accept your current position. Accepting the ego as it is, "here and now" is the gateway to the Self.

Opening to the Heart is not a question of spiritual level. There is no state to reach. Truth is beyond "high" and "low". These categories belong to the ego-mind only. Trying to be perfect is still the game of ego. You are already perfect. Simply open to what is within your field of perception. Open to the truth of what is "here and now". Truth is the Door. It does not matter what your inner state is (for example: a state of bliss or depression). What matters is being aware and accepting what is "here and now". This brings you beyond bliss or depression to the Source of your being.

You are already what you are looking for. The sky exists independently of the clouds. Yet, the sky welcomes all sorts of clouds without distinction, whether they are white, pink or grey. Similarly, Self-realisation is the acceptance of all types of thoughts. The mind is open like the space. Accepting, for example, the absence of serenity is true peace. Thoughts come but the mind does not resist them. Opening to the Heart is not about eliminating the clouds. It is about welcoming them. When no clouds disturb you at all, you are perfectly realised and wise. However, do not fall into the trap of looking for this type of perfection. Be open-minded. This is enough. By seeing and recognising your ego imperfections, you return to your natural state of perfection. Opening to truth is the gateway to the Heart.

The Heart has already completely accepted the ego. Like this, everybody is already forgiven and has never ceased being so. Only some minds resist their shadows. How can you know if you resist your ego? As long as you reject the ego of others, you do not accept your own ego. Simply surrender and accept your vulnerability. Drop your defence mechanisms and instead, develop a good sense of humour. Do not take yourself too seriously.

As a Yoga teacher, I see how it is sometimes difficult to surrender to what *is*. In each posture, there is no need to excel or to try to reach the perfect final pose. It is enough to relax and accept your limitations. It is actually in this state of non-resistance that body and mind relax and open. It is the same in actual life. When your mind does not resist the ego, all boundaries disappear. Yoga, in its original meaning of Union, opening to the Heart, is always "here and now", just the way you are, with your Light and your shadows, as the sky (space) embracing the clouds.

The Heart: Symbiosis Between the Inner and the Outer Reality

What is inside oneself manifests outside. Therefore, if I am asked "How can I find love and peace in my life?" I would answer thus: love and peace is who you truly are. Never doubt it. This can never be taken away from you. Now, in this life, simply do your best for love and peace. Do it while respecting your inner nature. Do not force yourself. It does not matter whether your participation is "big" or "small". Taking care of your family or looking after your garden is as respectable as building hospitals or retreating to a monastery.

Listen to your inner voice. Do what you feel is right and true for you, without expecting anything in return. Do not be attached to outcomes. Like this, you welcome true love and peace in your life.

We all wish to return "Home". The longing for love and peace, even when intense, is natural. The stream naturally finds its way to the ocean. On the other hand, the ego tends to follow the spiritual stream for its own sake only. So before following any stream, ask yourself the following questions: "What are my true intentions? Do I want to prove something or do I really want to help myself and/or other people? Does my project feel natural or is it the result of ambition and fears? What does my inner voice say?" Listen to this voice. This is how existence can help you and support you. Existence helps you anyway but if you listen to your mind, its help may take the form of a "stick" (the boomerang effect). Choices are clear. Listen to your heart.

Healing one's mind is also healing others. The inner reality has repercussions on the outer world. If someone holds a flashlight in a dark room, the light automatically reveals the way out. Inner peace is a precious gift. It is a drop of crystal-clear water that resonates in the entire ocean. Often, when there is a scientific discovery somewhere in the planet, the same discovery happens almost simultaneously on the other side of the planet. All information diffuses automatically. It is like waves being produced when the wind blows. The more people realise their true nature, the more Light spreads effortlessly and peacefully around the world. Several individuals realising their true nature can lead to a global shift in consciousness. If the inner reality has an impact on the outer world, in parallel, taking care of the outer world has repercussions on the inner self.

"What happens to the animals in the seas happens to us,
men and women.
What happens to the forests happens to us in our bodies,
since our bodies like the trees are made of the same earth.
Are not our bodies moving clay forms endowed with intelligence?

A conscientious effort at healing the earth
would manifest as the ultimate healing of our own bodies. "[14]

This world is supported by nature, animals and, of course, by peaceful and enlightened spirits. Consequently, let us not forget to be grateful to this "outer world" and to treat it with the respect it deserves. This is actually complete Self-respect.

Keeping an Open Mind

Keeping an open Heart is keeping an open mind. Some situations in life may have the effect of closing your mind. Here are a few keys that can help you keep your mind open and peaceful.

The Key of Understanding

Each time you reject certain aspects of yourself or others, remember this: *"What I don't love about myself is just my "wound". It is not who I am. Truly, I am Love."* And *"What I don't love about others is just their "wound". It is not who they are. Truly, everyone is Love."*

The Key of Sensitivity

Each time your heart does not feel at peace, remind yourself that it is because it does not feel satisfied. You can nourish and satisfy your heart by *being sensitive to your own needs and to the needs of others.* Some people never forget to satisfy their needs but they do not consider the needs of others. Consequently, they may feel indifferent or "empty" in a negative way. Other people take excessively care of

---

[14] Message received in an email forwarded by my friend Annamalai.

others while forgetting their own needs. As a result, there may be the feeling of a burden. Therefore, it is important to find the happy medium that is appropriate to your heart. This naturally evolves according to your opening to the Heart. For some, the opening is so wide that helping others without expecting anything in return is never a burden. Nonetheless, it is clear that you should not force yourself. Simply respect your nature. Nature has different rhythms and seasons. Sometimes, you need to take care of your own self and sometimes, it is the time to take care of others.

When you respect your nature, your heart is pure. It is not under the influence of conditioning. It may not be appreciated as a "big heart", but it is a pure heart. In this way, love is the freedom to be yourself. This love always brings harmony.

The Key of Humour

Instead of resisting the ego, why not recognise that *ego is the same in all of us*. What a relief! There is no need to pretend anything or to compare: "My ego is better than yours"! You are not your body. You are the Heart. And the Heart holds the totality of existence and all aspects of ego. Pure Consciousness is within every form. It is useless to point at others. Develop instead a good sense of humour!

The Key of Total Trust

Each time you are not satisfied with your life, remember that *everything is perfect the way it is*. Be confident and patient. Everything happens for a reason. When you do not feel clear about what decision to make, just be patient. When you really don't know what to do, wait until life shows you the way or until clarity comes.

Basically, every difficulty is a gift. Difficulties are there to make you stronger and more open-minded. They are there to show you how your mind is deceitful. Also, do not forget that what seems to be a misfortune today can actually turn out to be an invaluable chance in the future. Without the ego and the illusion of chains, would you know how to "free" yourself and enjoy your freedom? Have faith no matter what. Do not doubt the divine force of love and truth, especially if you have to face injustice. Love and truth will manifest. Nonetheless, absolute faith does not mean blind faith. Keep being vigilant. You are totally safe.

Finally, some people have irrational fears, superstitions or believe in "evil spirits". There is nothing to fear and nothing can affect you when you trust life and yourself. Are you afraid of yourself? Welcome the truth and return to inner silence. Wish heartily for Light (for your own self and others). This dispels all darkness.

The Key of Free Expression

Free expression is preferable to shutting down. Because of prejudices, you may close yourself off from certain people without even trying to know them. However, *if you feel free to express your opinion, being open to others is not frightening.* Do not be afraid of meeting life. Can you say "yes" to life if you close yourself off from its experiences?

Free expression is also preferable to defensive behaviour. Sometimes you may be afraid of losing face or damaging your reputation. Consequently, you may adopt a defensive or accusative attitude: "It is only their fault." In general, this behaviour does not bring openness and harmony. Finally, if you choose to say nothing, you may feel frustrated and may close yourself off even more. Each time this happens, remember this: *"Whatever the situation, I clearly explain my point of view and facts, without being defensive or aggressive".* You can thus remain open and peaceful.

53

Meeting Your "Wound"

The fact of seeing your "wound" can also help you keep your heart open. Some "wounds" are deep and hidden. Pain may take the form of indifference or a very friendly and funny mask. Whatever mask is on your face, dare to see it. One day, you may be surprised to see many tears flowing. Meeting your "wound" is meeting your Self.

Usually, the most spontaneous way to heal, when we get hurt, is to express emotions and anger. However, this may have unpleasant consequences that can be avoided. There are more respectful and gentle ways to heal. For example, the practice of Self-enquiry can help you meet your "wound" in the gentlest way. When you meet and observe the ego, it dissolves. Self-enquiry is also self-healing.[15]

Practice of Self-enquiry

Find who you truly are.
From this space, observe the "I" thought that disturbs you
as well as the emotions and the sensations in your body,
until all resistance ceases.

.

For example, if you are disturbed by some people who talk loudly around you and the thought "I want silence now" is in your mind, return to the Source. Welcome your thought, your negative emotions and the sensations in your body until they dissolve. Then, let your heart guide you to find a solution. Let us take another example. If thoughts like "I have a job interview" or "I have an exam to pass" disturb your mind, do not try to chase your fears away. On the contrary, open to them. Remember, it is always okay to feel the way

---

[15] A beautiful demonstration of this practice is given by Miranda Macpherson, satsang, Tiruvannamalai.

you feel "here and now". Open to the sensations in your body (belly, chest, throat or back). Breathe deeply to go through your emotions and your resistance. By not resisting what is "here and now", you return to the Source. This Source can also be called "stillness", "silence" or "openness". This is simply *You* without the interference of the ego. This is your refuge because nothing can affect this Presence.

Life regularly shows you what you resist. What are your knots? What disturbs you? What are your fears? Some thoughts cause you to feel negative emotions, uneasiness or discomfort. You may feel a contraction, a kind of closing, a sudden sensation of heat or cold. Instead of ignoring or avoiding these emotions and sensations, meet them completely. *By not resisting what is present "here and now" within your mind and body, you absorb your "wound".* Like this, you can heal yourself of all sorts of diseases. Believe in self-healing.

Let us play a game. If all the people you meet in your life have the ability to see absolutely everything about you, even your deepest secrets, would you be ashamed? Ego is active when you feel embarrassed, when you have irrational fears and when you cannot be at peace with someone. I now invite you to answer the questions below in order to identify your "wound" and heal it.

1. *What are you blamed for? Does it disturb you?*

2. *What do you reject about yourself? What embarrasses you?*

3. *What do you reject in others? Who do you reject?*

4. *What do you reject in the world? Which political, religious or historical characters disturb you?*

5. *What are your fears?*

Practice Self-enquiry. Find who you are. From this space, observe all disturbing thoughts and emotions until they dissolve. In daily life, each time you feel a resistance in your mind or a contraction in your body, return to the Source (the open and neutral observer). Do not get carried away by what disturbs you. Watch the content of your mind, without judging it, until all resistance ceases.

Here are a few other simple healing techniques:

When someone really disturbs you, write a letter to the person (without sending it). Express in this letter all that disturbs you, without holding back or trying to be correct and polite. Express all your dissatisfaction and disappointment, all your anger, maybe even your hate. By simply writing down your "wound" and grievances on paper, they don't get registered in your mind. Like this, the "wound" loses its power to manifest outside. Then, forget about it. Observe how your anger disappears in the hours or days following. Now, your mind is open and free again. So wait and write before letting the anger out.

To free yourself from pain, listen to your body. What does it want to do: cry, scream, lament, stretch in a certain way, shake and move all around, jump or dance? Let your body freely express itself.

When some relationships or situations are not easy, imagine the person or the situation that disturbs you. Breathe deeply while raising your chest. Breathe from the heart (middle of the chest) until you feel no resistance. Then your heart is open again. Forgive and forget.

There are many techniques and many professionals to help you heal your inner "wound". Follow your intuition.

You, who bathe every morning in the sunlight,
Show yourself equal, open to your inner light,
Stop hiding yourself,
Stop defending yourself,
Stop protecting yourself,
Stop building a fortress of knowledge,
Simply know who you are.
You have nothing else to do: be true.

Know yourself.
Know your shadows.
Know your masks.
Know your lies.
Know your fears.
Know your pride.

Dear key of honesty,
Oh! How precious you are.
When nothing remains hidden under the sun, See,
How its radiance shines forth and reveals who you are.
Light showers on you with grace and forgiveness.
Don't lose time, don't run in oblivion. Take some rest.
Truth unveiling will dissipate what you faced.
And Truth is right in your heart.

Wake-up!

The love for Truth reveals the truth of Love.

Chapter 5: Inner Reconciliation

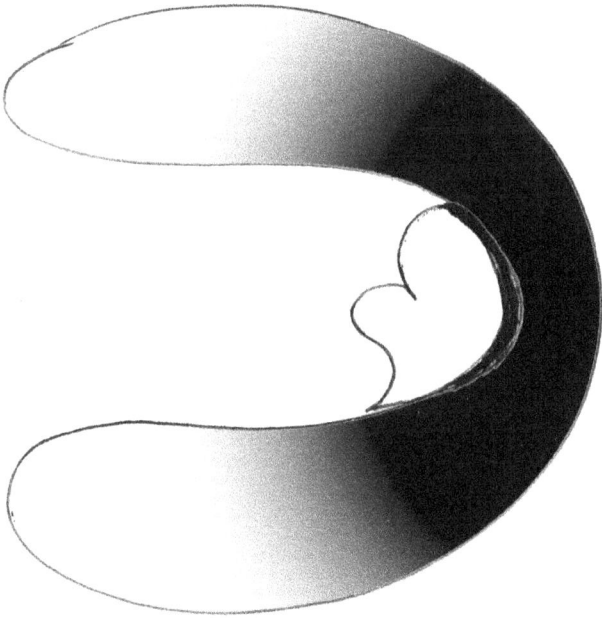

The Diamond in the Box

Spirituality is paradoxical. Everything is simple yet may seem complicated. Some people advise knowing the ego. Others claim this to be futile as ego has no reality. Only Pure Consciousness is real. However, is it easy to be Pure Consciousness, or Love, in daily life?

In truth, there is no problem. Yet, some minds have many "problems". Should you then pay attention to your ego or should you not?

By observing the ego, it dissolves. Yet, awareness of the ego is required for this. Is this awareness easy to gain?

It is also said that reaching the goal is having no goal. True peace has no expectation. Yet, every action done with a sincere intention brings a fruitful outcome. What can you do then? How can you gain clarity through the mist of paradoxes?

The Heart, like a diamond, is eternally pure but it is in a box (the mind). This box is either open or closed. How is it in your case?

1) The box is open or relatively open.
You can believe that you are the diamond. You are reconciled with your ego and you do not resist the truth. In general, fears, selfish desires and guilt do not influence you. You are usually in a good mood and honest. Your heart guides you. Therefore, it is not necessary for you to know your shadows. One day, grace (Light) will dissolve all of them. Simply remember who you truly are. Keep trusting the natural responses that spring out from you. Listen to your inner voice. Be aware, though, of your subtle ego. Do not take yourself too seriously. Keep being open to truth and you will find freedom.

2) The box is closed or relatively closed.
Fears, selfish desires and guilt influence you. In this case, you need to pay attention to the box (the mind) in order to open it. Here, ego is the Gateway. You have to know it in order to

reconcile with it. You have to be sufficiently conscious of what you resist in order to maintain your openness. In this respect, this chapter is of great help. It accelerates the process of awareness and inner reconciliation. When you are conscious of your ego and reconciled with it, your mind rests effortlessly in the Heart.

Peaceful people are generally open, spontaneous and joyful. Simply see to what category you belong (open or closed box). Can you bypass the forest of shadows or do you have to cross it (to do the Self-enquiry exercises listed in this chapter)? If you belong to the second category, I would like to add a few more points. First, do not feel "bad" to belong to this category. Remember that ego is not who you truly are. You simply carry within yourself a "programme" that you do not like. If you wish to, you can learn to stop judging this "programme" in order to free yourself from its influence.

There may be some aspects of the ego that you cannot see, simply because it is not yet the right time. You may not be ready to accept and integrate the consequences of awakening to truth. Just like the seasons, individuals have their own rhythms. It makes no sense to try to make the summer fruits ripen during spring. Follow your inner voice. Generally, I would recommend reading this chapter slowly, step by step. We all have different stages of development. Depending on how strongly you identify with ego, you need more or less time to reconcile with it. Nothing should be anticipated or forced. While opening to truth, it is likely that what is superficial in your life becomes subject to change. Are you ready for change? If you cling to what you believe or value as precious, opening to truth may be difficult. On the contrary, if openness, surrender and trust prevail, change can happen as gently as possible.

Some people have developed strong defence mechanisms and mental habits such as guilt and self-hate, and so Light (or Truth) is disturbing or frightening. This is normal because in the presence of light, shadows are automatically revealed. As long as there is guilt and identification with ego, truth is feared. If this is the case for you, respect your inner state. Do not force anything. Wait until "the red light turns to green". How do you feel inside? Do you feel strong and trusting or do you have many fears? In the latter case, I advise you to start by doing, slowly and carefully, the Self-enquiry exercises relating to fears.[16]

Some people may not be able to consider themselves lovable right away. They may not believe that their true nature is love. However, nothing can be truer. Everyone is love and deserves to be loved. Leave the past behind. Simply see your real beauty and avoid repeating the same mistakes. If this is not possible at the beginning, understand that this is natural. Babies only learn to walk after many attempts. Give time the time to heal you. If you keep your mind open to healing, life will help you because life is completely One with you. When you cannot believe that your true nature is love, start by trying your best for peace and love in your life. But do not force yourself. Respect your inner voice. This will quickly help you reconcile with yourself. Lift your head. Believe in your own beauty. Life loves you.

Other people may believe that they are already perfectly at peace with themselves. Is it true? They may be misled by their own serene or loving appearance. In order to help you identify whether the subtle ego is leading you or not, allow me to ask you the following questions:

Are you spontaneously open to any type of people, without prejudice? Do you have very little inclination towards criticisms? Can you accept being seen as a very ordinary person, not very interesting to others? Can you be alone without distractions? Can you keep your heart open while others misjudge you? Can you accept injustice against yourself? Can you accept looking ridiculous and being ridiculed? Do you follow your inner voice, irrespective of people's opinions? Can you take life just the way it is when it

---

[16] At the beginning of "Self-enquiry No.1" as well as "Self-enquiry No. 6 and 7".

does not meet your expectations? Can you quickly adapt to any situation? Can you keep quiet around arrogant people? Can you strongly react when necessary? Can you accept being the loser? Can you accept being the winner? Can you prevent irrational fears from ruling your life?

If you answer "yes" to all these questions, I believe self-reconciliation is complete. But again, do not forget that what truly matters is meeting the truth of what is "here and now". There is nothing else to reach. Yoga (Union - non-duality) is not about achieving the perfect final pose. Yoga is simply about self-acceptance "here and now". For this, humility and honesty are sufficient. Being open to truth is sufficient. Nonetheless, this openness requires a conscious heart (sensitivity) or a conscious mind (awareness). When you are not conscious of your behaviour, it is clear that truth is unnoticed. For example, if you do not realise that your vehicle blocks the access to a shop, you cannot understand the legitimate annoyance of the merchant. If you believe that you are conscious while the subtle ego influences you, you deceive yourself. How can you be conscious?

In order to gain clarity and awareness, I give a detailed account of "I" thoughts in the next pages. These pages help reconcile with the different aspects of the ego and pass through the gates of consciousness (five main gateways).[17] In this sense, this chapter is an initiation. Each gateway corresponds to different aspects of the ego and to a body part.[18] Body and mind are interdependent. Depending on your state of mind, energy flows more or less freely in your body.

---

[17] This chapter describes only five gateways, corresponding to five chakras (psycho-physiological centres). They are the basic foundations for the opening of individual consciousness to Universal Consciousness. The sixth and seventh chakras are studied separately in the last chapter of this book (chapter 7).

[18] Each body part corresponds to a chakra. Chakras are energy centres that relate to a body part: endocrine glands. Each chakra is associated with personal qualities (grounding, sociability, etc.). Joy Gardner-Gordon, *Pocket Guide to Chakras,* Book Faith India, Delhi.

This also has an influence on the outside world. When the mind is balanced, the body is healthy and life is harmonious. Hence, by identifying your mental "knots" (what you resist inwardly), your overall personal situation improves. Foundations are also laid for a greater opening. Clarity is a transformational tool.

If clarity is important, it should not be taken too seriously either. Our real destination is the Heart. The Heart is reached when the mind is both light and respectful. Be sensitive. For example, if your mind is clear, do not impose your clarity on others. This could be disrespectful. If someone has a physical problem, do not immediately express your views about the possible mental cause of the problem. Respect people's sensitivity and boundaries. Question also your opinions. They may be wrong despite all apparent evidence. In other words, I would say that it is important not to play the "psychologist" or the "spiritual adviser". Simply feel the situation and listen to your friend without your ego being in the way in the name of love, spirituality or healing. Understand also that in some cases, love is not welcome. This should be respected. Let your heart express itself and not your ego. For example, avoid saying: "You should be grateful to have this problem because it helps you see what you are resisting". Do you think this is what your friend wants to hear? Let us keep being humane, sensitive, open and warm. It is only from a place of love and respect that clarity is welcome.

If you decide to do the following Self-enquiry exercises, it is important that you respect your own pace. Take breaks. Take time to breathe. Slowly integrate the thoughts that disturb you. Depending on your level of awareness and integration, each section can take more or less time: one hour, one day, one week, one month or a few months. The whole process can even take years. You can stop for a while and then practice again. This really helps stabilise the inner state and observe the behaviour change in actual life. In the course of your reading and practice, feel what pace is right for you. Read more attentively the gateway that corresponds to your body/mind "weaknesses". Where do you usually have pain or physical stress? What disease do you tend to have? What is the body part involved?

65

Because each gateway relates to a body part and personal qualities, you can easily identify the gateway that is more appropriate for your practice.

I intentionally use the "you" form in the following pages. This is not to point my finger at you or to accuse you. It is simply a way to show you when your mind gets disturbed and identifies with ego. Whenever you resist the truth about your ego, practice Self-enquiry: "Who am I?" Are you your thoughts, your emotions, your feelings, your body? All of these are within you but they are not truly you. You are the Presence that recognises them. When you find who you are, you can watch your ego with detachment. Resistance ceases. While reading the next pages, identify in the italic parts the "I" thoughts and the examples that relate to you. For each case, practice Self-enquiry until there is no more resistance. Like this, you can very gently remove the veils of the ego.

Practice of Self-enquiry

Find who you truly are.
From this space, observe the "I" thought that disturbs you,
as well as the emotions and the sensations in your body,
until all resistance ceases.

"May you be given…
For every storm, a rainbow.
For every tear, a smile.
For every care, a promise
And a blessing in each trial.
For every problem life sends,
A faithful friend to share with.
For every sigh, a sweet song
And an answer for each prayer."[19]

---

[19] Poem received in an email forwarded by my friend Annamalai.

The First Gateway

Mooladhara Chakra
(between the anus and the genitals)
Grounding, Relationship to the Body, to the Outer World and
to Practical Affairs

Self-enquiry No.1: Self-acceptance

The first chakra is very important. It is your greatest foundation. The opening of this chakra depends on the unconditional love received during childhood and the impressions left by the outer world at that time. Your first life experiences have conditioned your inner strength and self-esteem. If there was little love during childhood or if you had traumatic experiences, you may feel the need to hold onto certain pillars to build self-esteem (the pillar of professional success, the pillar of money, the pillar of culture, the pillar of sentimental love or the pillar of the good person).

Are you dependent on a pillar for self-love? Which one? Without this pillar, what would you fear? Do not be afraid of the words defining your fear. It is not because you name your fear that it will manifest. On the contrary, the fear that is named dissolves. Resistance may eventually manifest the fear (law of attraction/repulsion[20]) but non-resistance sets you free from fears.

When a fear crosses your mind, practice Self-enquiry. Return to your inner Presence (the open and neutral observer). From this space, watch your fear. Repeat inwardly the name of your fear "I am afraid of" and breathe from your belly until the fear dissolves.

Your real nature (you as Presence) can never worry because it absorbs and dissolves all worries. Also, remember that this Presence is not limited to you. It is within every form. This is why life is sacred and protects you. Do not worry. Remain peaceful and open. Let

---

[20] Everything is energy, even thoughts. Energy obeys the law of attraction/repulsion. Consequently, the mind attracts what it resists until resistance ceases.

decisions, words and actions come from this space of openness. This is where you find your refuge and your freedom.

If your past still disturbs your mind, simply look and open to disturbing thoughts and emotions. For example, if you were not wanted or loved as a child, observe the content of your mind: "I lacked love", "I was not loved", "I don't love my parents" or "I hold a grudge against them". Observe your negative feelings: "I feel disappointed, sad, angry or hateful". All your thoughts and emotions are legitimate. Do not judge them. Do not try to eliminate them. Return to the Source. Practice Self-enquiry. From this place of stillness, watch the thoughts and the negative feelings that disturb you until they dissolve.

If you believe you lack self-love, watch the content of your mind: "I don't love myself" or "I don't love my body". Return to the Source. Observe your thoughts, your feelings of embarrassment and self-dislike until they dissolve. Observe directly that you, as Presence, never lack love nor need anything. Your true nature is already perfectly peaceful and loving. Bliss is your natural state. But remember: to find bliss in daily life, do not look for it. Simply welcome your shadows. For example, if your attitude in life is: "I want to find peace so I will avoid all disturbing people, family life and social events", you may have to wait for a while before finding real peace. On the contrary, if your attitude is: "I will naturally go with the flow of life and face what I have to face", then peace is "here and now". Choices are clear.

Peace is present when you embrace the present moment as it is. Bliss is simply the contentment of the mind that does not pretend anything, does not expect anything and does not look for anything special. The mind is also detached from what is extraordinary. What goes up comes down. Therefore, find your centre and stay there. This centre is the Heart. It is your original mind: neutral, balanced, open and pure (uncontaminated by hasty judgments and worries). From this Source, joy, compassion and forgiveness arise naturally.

Self-enquiry No.2: Self-acceptance

Identification with ego is the main reason for lack of self-acceptance. Similarly, identifying others with ego is the main reason for lack of acceptance of others. However, when you practice Self-enquiry, you clearly see that you are truly not the ego and that actually, no one else is really the ego. Compassion comes from understanding. Nonetheless, the understanding that you are not the cloud but space (Pure Consciousness), should not be an excuse to deny the existence of clouds. It is important to see them. It is important to open to the truth about your "ego programme." How could you open to the Self if you reject some aspects of your ego, even if they are basically untrue? The small self is the gateway to the Self.

When you do not resist what is "here and now", there is no duality. Your mind is at peace. For example, you can recognise in a detached way that the programme "egoism" is in you and may have affected some people. Truth is the gateway to the Heart. Truth is also the gateway to health. Usually, a disease is the manifestation of a resistance to truth. Consequently, by identifying what you resist, your mind and body heal. I offer here a summary of the ego tendencies the mind generally resists the most. This summary takes the form of questions. For each question, practice Self-enquiry until all resistance ceases. Proceed according to the following model:

1. Read the question.
For example: "Are you insensitive?"

2. Immediately practice Self-enquiry.
Who are you truly? You are not the ego but the Presence that recognises the ego. You are the open and neutral observer. From this base, you can welcome the truth about your ego.

3. Welcome the truth about your ego.

Is there insensitivity in you? What are the consequences of this insensitivity? Open to the disturbing "I" thoughts and emotions (for example: "I am insensitive" and "I may have hurt this person"). Watch the "I" thoughts until they dissolve. Ask for forgiveness in your heart.

Take your time. In total, there are 27 questions and they represent the inner "load", the ego programme that is within all of us in a more or less active way. For instance, answer only one question a day or one question a week. Choose the pace that is the most convenient for you. Do not read all the questions at once. While doing your practice, breathe from your belly to the chest each time thoughts and emotions disturb you. Let them dissolve. Free yourself from the ego burden.

List of questions

1. Are you selfish (for example: you only consider your personal interests)?
2. Are you insensitive (for example: you do not realise how your words or behaviour affect others)?
3. Are you indifferent (for example: you do not pay much attention to people or listen to them)?
4. Are you vain (for example: you speak too highly of your way of being or doing things)?
5. Are you rigid (for example: you are unable to question yourself)?
6. Are you arrogant (for example: you impose your opinions on other people, you presume you know better and you feel superior)?
7. Are you hard (for example: you get accusative or critical whenever you are confronted with resistance)?
8. Are you disrespectful (for example: you do not really respect those who are different from you)?

9. Are you excessively proud (for example: you are unable to recognise your mistakes)?

10. Are you mean (for example: you humiliate some people or you put them down, even subtly)?

11. Are you greedy (for example: you want "more and better, again and again")?

12. Are you ambitious (for example: you look for power for its own sake, even in subtle ways)?

13. Are you domineering (for example: you want to control)?

14. Are you dissatisfied (for example: you complain a lot)?

15. Are you cunning (for example: you invent excuses or stories to justify your behaviour)?

16. Are you a liar (for example: you prefer to lie rather than face reality and take responsibility)?

17. Are you manipulative (for example: you play with people's hearts or you take advantage of others)?

18. Are you self-interested (for example: you offer a gift in order to get something else in return)?

19. Are you false (for example: you play the good person but you criticise people behind their back)?

20. Are you corrupt (for example: you let yourself be influenced by values other than general well-being)?

21. Are you insecure (for example: you under-estimate yourself, you are clumsy, you think that problems are generally your fault or you have many doubts)?

22. Are you weak (for example: you are afraid of losing your reputation, you are afraid of being ridiculed or you are afraid of being uninteresting and boring, you worry about what others think)?

23. Are you ashamed of yourself (for example: you feel embarrassed, you are afraid of disturbing others and you feel guilt)?

24. Are you difficult (for example: you play the victim)?

25. Are you jealous (for example: you compare yourself with others or you do not accept other people's happiness and success)?
26. Are you stingy (for example: you do not like to share)?
27. Are you fearful (for example: you let fears influence your behaviour)?

So what? If your ego has such and such characteristics, there are definitely reasons for them. *Forgive yourself.* Make peace with your mind. Who is truly responsible for your ego? The past is simply in your cells and memories. It is not your fault. Do not feel guilty. Do not try to radically eliminate your ego tendencies in daily life. Continue to recognise and accept them. Accept them also in other people, while of course behaving naturally (with respect for others but also for yourself).

*Here are the four main ego tendencies: **"expectations"**, **"need to prove your worth"**, **"need to blame and criticise"** and **"fear of losing"**. Remember them. Each time they cross your mind, observe them until they dissolve. Do not identify with your ego. Remain open.*

The work of inner reconciliation that you have just done is basically a summary of the remaining pages. So it is up to you now to continue reading this chapter or not. The following pages will give you a deeper awareness in your daily life. Awareness is the transformational tool. Nothing else is needed.

Self-enquiry No.3: Self-acceptance

When identification with ego is strong, the mind cannot detach from it in order to face it. Opening to truth is not yet possible. Self-defence mechanisms prevent some people from doing so. The first thing some people reject about themselves is their vulnerability.

If you are afraid of being bare and vulnerable, open to your fears: "I am afraid of being totally open and vulnerable". Practice Self-enquiry. Find who you really are. From this place, watch your fear as well as the feeling of vulnerability and fragility until they dissolve. See that your real strength is the total acceptance of vulnerability.

In fear of vulnerability you may wear a mask. We all wear a mask to a greater or lesser extent. We also change our mask according to situations and circumstances. What is your mask: the good person, the funny clown, the strong one, the cool guy, the wise, courageous, intelligent, cultivated, generous, hardworking, loving, calm, authentic, spiritual or even the hard or cold person? Can you reconcile with your mask and welcome it? Practice Self-enquiry and see what your real face is. Understand also that as long as your mask does not disturb anyone, it is not a problem. You can be playful.

In certain cases, identification with a character is so strong that questioning it would be unbearable. It is not yet possible to see the lies and the game of your ego. This has to be respected. Time slowly lifts the veils.

Has the use of "you" disturbed you in the previous pages? When someone points at your ego, do you feel annoyed? If so, return to the Source. Open to your feelings of annoyance until they dissolve.

How do you feel when you are not held in the esteem you should be, for example, as the Pure Self? Can you accept wrong ideas about yourself? Do you feel a certain kind of injustice? Do you have a subtle feeling of superiority? Do you have the need to prove your superiority? Do you take yourself too seriously? Remember, what you think comes from your ego programme only. Find who you are and stay there. Open to the truth about your ego and let the clouds dissolve. See that Pure Consciousness is "Nothing", a simple Presence. Is this not the greatest freedom?

When vulnerability is not accepted, you may become aggressive, critical or accusative towards the people who dare to tackle your ego. Then, you are like the hunter with the trap. You catch every sign that proves you are right. You project all your mistakes on others. If you are smart, this can be very deceptive. Find who you are and welcome the truth: "I lie to others and to myself". Let disturbing feelings dissolve. Do not identify with ego.

Self-enquiry No.4: Self-acceptance

There may also be resistance to truth (or ego) if you believe you belong to the "good" side. The "good" and "cool" person, the intellectual, the moralist, the idealist, the spiritual person may be trapped by their values or their knowledge. For example, politically or spiritually correct people may interpret criticisms or "judgments" as evidence of a problem. Criticisms can be simple statements of facts rather than signs of rejection. Whenever you react hastily against what you call "closed or judgmental minds", are you so sure to be truly open yourself?

What are your values? Do they prevent you from opening to what is different? How do you welcome criticisms? Do you easily criticise people who are not like you or seem to be less open, cool, good or pure than you? Often, without even noticing it, you compare and feel jealous. Can you accept this? Can you also accept your lack of openness? As you know, these tendencies only come from your ego programme. Do not feel "bad". Return to the Source and watch your clouds until they dissolve.

In fear of vulnerability, you may also have trouble tolerating softness, friendliness and fragility in others. You may easily interpret these qualities as false or weak. Simply watch the doubt in your mind and see whether falseness and weakness are not shadows you reject within yourself. Know who you truly are and welcome the truth. Watch your clouds until they dissolve.

If you cannot stand strong characters or firm and authoritative behaviour, you may hastily judge them as aggressive or unloving. Simply be aware that you may be wrong. See whether anger and "lack of love" are not shadows you reject within yourself. Observe your inner feelings and find peace.

Simply open to the truth about your ego. This will help you build your true inner pillar and flow with life in a natural way.

Tell me friend, do you know where your happiness resides?
Do you know how to build your inner pillar and see pain subside?
There is a place of stillness within where you simply feel well,
A sea undisturbed by the swell.
Winds will blow.
Fall and winter you will know.
But this pillar will hold you up and let you flow.
It will soothe all your pains, don't you know?
This inner pillar is made of peace.
This inner space is freedom.
When the mind is at ease,
There is freedom from dependencies.
Do you know what you need?
Do you know what you cannot do without
And which disturbs you, in and out?
The need for approval, for self-assertion?
The need for strong sensations, friends and crowds:
Self-oblivion?
The need to be admired and to prove one's charm?
The need for money? Can't you let go and disarm?
The need for seduction and childish tricks?
The need to parade and appear fantastic?
The need for certain ties, falsely reassuring?
The need to conform, limiting your flowing?
The need for the norm makes you superficial indeed.
Needs, needs, needs...
You make happiness a conditional seed.
But when your inner pillar gets straight,
It takes you out of your distress,
It is your natural awareness – no need for effort,
It leads you to peace within, our eternal Harbour.

Self-enquiry No.5: Acceptance of the World

Faced with the limitations of consumer-society, the way politics operate, the conditions of underprivileged women, children and dropouts or the way nature is treated, you can easily feel revolted and negatively charged against a certain order of the world. However, negative attitude will not solve anything and will only add more misery to the already negative load. Only inner peace creates outer peace. There is only one long-lasting solution for peace and justice in the world and it is self-reconciliation: fully accepting yourself and the world as it is today. Out of this acceptance, simply act naturally in the outer world. For example, if your heart (not your mind) tells you to do your best for a certain cause, go ahead and do it. But do it with awareness, for a cause and not against a certain order. This attitude changes everything ("I will do my best to help these people", "I will do my best for such a cause", "I will do my best to be a responsible consumer", "I will do my best to protect nature", "I will do my best to protect animals", and "I will do my best for peace").

On the other hand, if your mind is in control ("I cannot stand this situation any longer", "punishment has to prevail" or "these people have to be given a good lesson"), do not listen to your mind. Find inner peace. Trust life. If justice has to be done, justice will be done. If you have to be personally involved in the defence of justice, you can now do it with inner peace, and not anger, as your guide. Also, if your heart does not feel involved in any cause, respect it. Pure Consciousness is beyond good and bad. Acting against your heart never brings harmony. Do not be afraid of moralists if they try to make you feel bad. Welcome them in your heart and be aware of their game. Be true to yourself. Truth is the door.

So, think about the world and accept it completely as it is: with all its negativity, wars, victims, injustice and pollution. Breathe from your chest until you find inner peace.

What disturbs you in the world? What is your battle? Which political, historical and religious characters do you have trouble accepting? Return to the Source. From there, watch all the thoughts that disturb you until all resistance ceases.

By "integrating" the world within, you heal yourself of the illusion of separation. You also give the world a chance to heal itself of its misery. With awareness and self-integration, we can stop the inner as well as the outer battles. This is part of evolution. Love, being a unifying factor, always prevails over division. The world is bound to heal and know peace.

Self-enquiry No.6: Irrational Fears

Some fears are natural. They are justified in the present moment. For example, you worry when your dog barks at night. On the other hand, some fears are not justified. They are irrational. They are the result of false beliefs and conditioning. For instance, you are afraid of studying philosophy because you may not get a good job in the future or, you want people to join your cause to "save" them (case of some missionaries). Ego is dominant in such cases because fears are dominant. There is no trust in one's Self and existence.

Think carefully about all your fears. Do you have fears in respect to your body, your health, the people you love, death, security? Return to the Source. Close your eyes. Repeat silently in your mind: "I am afraid of..." until all feelings of fear dissolve. Breathe from the belly. Do not forget that it is not because you name your fear that it will manifest. On the contrary, naming your fear sets you free from it. In any case, whether you have fears or not, do not worry. Life is sacred and protects you.

Here are a few other examples of common fears: "I am afraid of not being loved", "I am afraid of indifference", "I am afraid of being vulnerable", "I am afraid of failure", "I am afraid of lacking money", "I am afraid of being manipulated", "I am afraid of losing". Return to the Source. Watch all "I" thoughts and emotions until they dissolve.

The greatest victory over fears is not being afraid of losing. When you can inwardly accept being the loser, what else to fear? There is no inner conflict. You are totally free. What is your battle? What are you afraid of losing: face, reputation, the things or relationships that are superficial in your life? What

*are you clinging to? Return to the Source. Go through your
fears until they dissolve.*

Self-enquiry No.7: Irrational Fears

Whenever you believe that you have lost contact with your true nature, you feel something is lacking. You may also feel greedy or anxious. You may look outside for what you already have inside. Remember who you truly are. Have faith in yourself and existence. Simply relax and life will bring you exactly what you need (not always what you think you need). Learn to enjoy the present moment and let the mystery of life unravel.

What are you greedy for? Do you have an uncontrollable eagerness to see, experiment, possess and always do more (whether it is while travelling, with your children, friends or at work)? Does this inner feeling of "lacking something" also make you possessive? What do you fear? What is your anguish like? Can you feel it within yourself? Return to the Source and watch all your clouds until they dissolve.

You may also be afraid of having fears. If so, remember that being afraid of something does not mean that you will automatically be confronted with your fear. The fear has to be deep and recurrent before it manifests itself. Simply practice openness and non-resistance towards the thoughts you reject. Close your eyes and repeat in your mind: "I am afraid of having fears" until all feelings of fear vanish. Do not worry. What you face inwardly cannot manifest outside. It stops the process of attraction and repulsion. This really sets you free.

What is there to be afraid of? Do not pay attention to your mind. Your thoughts are just like clouds. They come and disappear. Why worry about a future that does not yet exist? Why hold fears from a past that is gone? Why have excessive fears of so-called "negative people"? These are only irrational fears, the non-acceptance of your ego. Every day is a new day, a rebirth. Return to your inner silence and directly experience that your real nature can never be affected.

Self-enquiry No.8: Irrational Fears

You may be afraid of yourself but also of all that is different from you. Paradoxically, even so-called religious or spiritual people may have this fear. Some of them protect themselves from people they consider impure, negative or simply different. However, as long as at your core, you are not the friend of the "untouchable", the Jew, the Muslim, the Hindu, the Christian, the Buddhist or the non-spiritual, how can you be the friend of your Self? How can you, in the name of God or in the name of oneness, exclude and reject? How can you, in the name of love, act against love? As long as you reject certain branches of your tree, you cut yourself off from your divine sap. We are all on our way to the realm of love and love is not exclusive and sectarian.

Do you reject and exclude in the name of God, purity or humanitarian values? Return to the Source and open to truth. Do not identify with ego. Watch all your thoughts and feelings until they dissolve.

Fears can also be strong in regard to material possessions and money. Material security is a reassuring pillar and some people get excessively attached to it.

What relationship do you have with material objects and money? Are you detached or strongly attached? Is money a means to proving your importance or your generosity to others? Is it a means to manipulate and exert power over others? Do you have a need to accumulate? Do you have difficulties sharing or giving? Do you doubt generous behaviour? Are you rather paranoid (easily believing one wants to rob or abuse you)? Or, do you spend without thinking, putting your own security at stake? Why do you reject money? Why on the contrary do you give it so much importance? Open to truth and return to the Source, your unshakable inner safety.

Money in itself is not a problem but your attitude towards money may be a problem. Do not create a taboo out of money. Do not have taboos about anything. The lighter your attitude towards everything, the less your life is influenced by attraction and repulsion.

Self-enquiry No.9: Irrational Fears

Let us also examine some common fears which may limit you. For example, you may have the tendency to postpone certain decisions. Often, the more you wait, the stronger the fear or the resistance. To overcome resistance and welcome all new life experiences is a wonderful opportunity to learn, grow and blossom. Why not "dive" into new experiences immediately? However, when you do not manage to do that, do not resist resistance! Do not force yourself.

Observe the fears and the thoughts that cross your mind (e.g. "I am not good enough for that" or "I am afraid of having to prove something"), until they dissolve.

There is also a common fear that may prevent you from meeting your true self. It is the fear of boredom. One day, a strange feeling suddenly overwhelmed a friend who visited a totally open house in the woods. This was the house of his dreams, the paradise that would fulfil him. However, fear took hold of him. What next? What happens when one is fulfiled?

Fulfilment may appear boring. Are you afraid of it? Do you fear it will lead you to the absence of desires and a monotonous life? Return to the Source and open to your fear until it dissolves. Welcome bliss.

To simply face yourself may appear scary, disturbing or annoying. The mental structure is so used to moving that when the movement stops, because you get close to something that totally fulfils you, you may take a step back out of fear of getting bored or becoming dull.

Can you accept and face your boredom? Whoever accepts boredom can never be bored. Can you also accept being seen as boring, uninteresting or ordinary? These fears show you how you may actually run away from yourself. Are you afraid of yourself? Pratice Self-enquiry. Return to inner peace and let it guide you.

When fears disappear, ego no longer "drives your vehicle". Your true nature is in command. The sunflower turns to the sun...Yet, change is a mere appearance along the thread of continuity.

The Second Gateway

Swadhisthana Chakra
(between the genitals and the navel)
Sociability, Friendship, Desires and Sexuality

Self-enquiry No.10: Acceptance of Others

As long as you are not reconciled with your ego, some people mirror what you reject. You project on them the shadows you do not accept within yourself. Here are some common projections:

For example, if you project on a person who is assertive a lack of humility, your pride may be repressed or personal qualities may not be completely expressed. If you do not accept "uninteresting or ordinary people", your own ordinariness may not be accepted. If criticism is not welcome, there may be self-doubt or the need for self-recognition. If you do not accept your own weaknesses or mistakes, you may reject the limitations of other people. If you do not like yourself, you may be aggressive or arrogant with others and see others so. Lack of self-love generally expresses itself as unfair judgments of others. If you recognise this tendency in you, do not feel "bad". This comes from your ego programme only. Simply be aware of your tendency to judge. Do not automatically trust your mind. Do not also believe in other people's judgments. They may be right, they may be wrong. Ego loves to criticise. Observe this tendency in you. Return to the Source and welcome your shadows until they dissolve.

The shadows that are projected on other people are personal and different. The reflection in the mirror is never absolutely symmetrical. If you cannot stand arrogant people, it does not mean that your own ego is arrogant. You may simply lack self-confidence. Therefore, it is important to be very careful with regard to any conclusion. Return to the Source. Watch the content of your mind without judging it until all clouds are gone. Also, do not believe that all your thoughts are the results of projections and false beliefs. You may be very innocent. In this case, ego does not influence you. Your heart does not reject anyone and you do not have any "bad" thoughts. You are generally detached from your perceptions (from what you see, hear and think). Your behaviour and your thoughts are natural. You are open but you also respect yourself and can defend yourself if it is necessary. Because of that, you may doubt your innocence. So each time "self-doubt" comes into your mind, return to the Source. Be aware of your doubt until it dissolves. Trust your spontaneity and your natural responses.

As we have seen before, "accepting others" should not make you fall into an unrealistic understanding of love and spirituality. The inner "yes" is not an obstacle to the outer "no". Keep being natural. See how parents behave with their children. Parents set limits and express disagreement and even anger when it is necessary. Yet, deep within, there is still the total understanding and unconditional acceptance of the children. So each time you do not know how to behave with someone, imagine that this person is your child (or someone very close). What would you do or say? Answers are very simple. Some people have the tendency to accept whatever comes in their life because "It is God's will". However, don't you think that Divine will is for you to free yourself from fears and guilt? Do not force yourself into false "good behaviour". Respecting yourself is another way of respecting others.

When you are trapped into false "good behaviour", return to the Source. Observe your fears and your guilt until they dissolve. Find inner silence and feel free to be yourself.

Naturally, we all have greater or lesser affinities with some people. We also have more or less understanding about each other. When the flow is not there, simply do what feels natural (e.g. ask for clarification, express your disagreement or gently detach). Respect your inner voice. This brings peace to everybody. In some cases, saying "no" is not a sign of rejection. It is a sign of self-respect. However, on occasions, saying "no" is not natural. If you reject someone just because this person belongs to a group of people you do not like, this is no longer natural.

Do you have automatic prejudices towards people who belong to a particular group, religion, political party or country? If so, return to the Source. See what your fears are and observe them until they dissolve. Remain open and let this openness be the source of your expression and behaviour.

Self-enquiry No.11: Desires and Expectations

Let us first specify that having needs and desires is natural as long as they do not hinder harmony. However, needs and desires can also bring expectations, dissatisfaction and stress in relationships. Happy people naturally have desires and preferences but they do not have expectations. If their needs are satisfied, all the better. If not, it is also fine. There may be temporary disappointment, sadness or even anger but joy is quick to return. On the contrary, when happiness strictly depends upon the satisfaction of needs, it can never be found. In this case, be aware of your *"needy mind"* and it will stop influencing you.

The "needy mind" tends to blame others or society for its dissatisfaction. If you have this tendency, observe it in your life. Each time the cloud "blame" crosses your mind, welcome it until it dissolves.

Expectations lead to dissatisfaction. The thought "I want it this way" often leads to stress (e.g. "I want silence now", "I want the waiter to serve me quickly" or "I want to be listened to"). When the cloud "I want" is loaded with expectation, impatience and annoyance, watch it until it dissolves. Return to inner peace and move from there. Let decisions and words come from this space of openness. Then, relationships improve. For example, you ask much more nicely to be served quickly. Aggressiveness disappears.

The "need to prove" can also lead to dissatisfaction. Do you have this tendency? If so, what do you need to prove: success, strength, intelligence, love or honesty? Each time the "need to prove" comes into your mind, return to the Source and watch it until it dissolves. Trust yourself and existence. Your true nature is already wonderful. You do not need to prove anything.

Self-enquiry No.12: Desires and Expectations

Some people feel the need to change their life. If this is the case for you, you may have good reasons for wanting this change. However, before making a decision, reflect on the following questions:

Do you really believe that you will be happier tomorrow if you change partner or job, if you have more money or if you move to another house? Have you not yet realised that after the excitement of all new experiences, come the same "problems"? Would it not be more sensible to have a good look at yourself first? Problems are in your mind. If they are not resolved there, they will keep on manifesting in your life.

For example, by wanting "always more and always better" or by postponing important moments in life, you may miss simple moments of happiness and the enjoyment of the present moment.

What prevents you from enjoying the present moment as it is? When the cloud "resistance" crosses your mind, watch it until it dissolves. Open to the present moment and to the flow of life. Surrender.

On the other hand, your desire for change may be very sincere and necessary. If so, what change is really needed? What can you do to bring about this change in the most harmonious way?

What prevents you from taking the necessary steps? What desires or expectations restrain you? What obstacles do you have to overcome? Watch the thoughts that limit you until they dissolve.

Let your inner sensitivity guide you to implement this change in the most harmonious way.

The more you get in touch with your inner silence, the more answers come naturally and clearly. Needs and expectations are perceived differently. When the mind is at peace, there is a distance from needs and expectations. Happiness is already there, inside you. You just have to feel it and drink it from your own well. So, whenever you go through difficult and "needy" times, take some time for yourself. Practice meditation, go for a walk in nature or stay alone for a while. Return to your inner silence and let it guide you.

Self-enquiry No.13: Flexibility of Mind

Happiness is the result of few expectations and much flexibility. What is your personal situation like?

If you tend to have mental or physical contractions, you may lack flexibility. Observe your mind. Each time you feel these contractions, be conscious of them and relax. Be open. For example, each time you feel a "knot" inside you that prevents you from flowing with life, from adapting to new situations or opening to different opinions, observe this "knot" until it dissolves. Go with the flow. Do you know what this knot is? Is it the fear of others, the fear of losing control, the fear of dropping your mask, the fear of vulnerability or the fear of being wrong and powerless? Do not forget who you really are. Your true nature is already perfect. The rest is just a movie on the screen. Do not be afraid of your ego. Face it peacefully until it disappears.

If intransigence and inflexibility is what you feel sometimes, be conscious of your feelings and let them dissolve. You may be too attached to your personality, your way of life or your values. For example, if your eating habits are very healthy, you may not want the company of someone who drinks beer, and vice versa. What is there to be taken so seriously? In any case, your true nature cannot be affected. So a bit of imperfection here and there does not matter much, does it?

Can you accept others being different? Can you accept others making mistakes and their ego being imperfect? Can you also accept your own ego being imperfect? Return to the Source. Watch your "clouds" until they dissolve. How is your mind now? It is open and it can accept differences and imperfections in the ways of thinking, speaking, doing and being. This is truly you. The acceptance of imperfections is true perfection. Maintain your openness in daily life.

Self-enquiry No.14: Flexibility of Mind

You may have experienced some "explosive" situations in the past. Remember well what these situations were in order to integrate them completely and to prevent their manifestation again.

Reflect carefully on the situations that push your buttons. Deactivate them. What is "unbearable" to you? Return to the Source. Watch all your clouds "unbearable situation" until they dissolve. Maintain your inner peace.

If you sometimes feel the following negative emotions: injustice, frustration, disappointment, anger or hate, return to the Source. Observe these emotions until they dissolve. Maintain your inner peace. Remember that peace is not the elimination of emotions ("I have to get rid of my emotions"). Peace is there when you welcome your emotions. Then, they naturally dissolve. Do not try to eradicate the ego. Accept it as it is, here and now. This is the most efficient way to prevent its influence.

As far as anger is concerned, I once heard an Indian story about a snake visiting a sage. The snake asked the sage how to live a happy life. The answer suggested was "Stop biting". The snake carried out this advice but soon got very hurt. Nobody was scared of him any longer and people were throwing stones at him. The snake went to the sage again for advice. The sage told him that he should not be submissive either. "Scare people away. Make some hissing noise but without biting. Like this, you will be respected and happy."

What is your anger like? Do you feel the need to attack or are you able to express your anger without hurting or blaming others? Return to the Source. Watch your cloud "need to attack" until it dissolves.

Can the "I" replace the "you" while expressing your anger? For example, instead of saying "You are annoying", you can say "I feel angry or sad when you..." Then, there is no direct offence and judgment. Disagreement ends more quickly.

Sometimes, anger needs to be strongly expressed and it may take the form of judgment. Free expression is healthy when it comes from the Source. This is sometimes the case of the anger of parents towards their children. The purpose is obviously not to hurt them but to make them clearly understand a point (after other means have failed). Be natural and do not be afraid of expressing yourself freely.

There is also a very good technique for expressing disagreement or anger. In turn, each person freely expresses his/her disagreement or anger, without being interrupted. There is nothing like getting anger off one's chest and being listened to. It is also enjoyable to observe that you can listen to someone's disagreement or anger without interfering. Then, there is room for openness again.

Can you listen to disagreement or anger without interfering? When the desire to interfere crosses your mind, watch it until it dissolves. Remain open, even in angry situations.

Sometimes, attempts to get along with certain individuals fail because there is simply a mismatch. Some ways of thinking and living correspond, some others don't. It is better to recognise this as soon as possible in order to prevent unnecessary misunderstandings or arguments. Without judging, gently distance yourself from such relations. Peace and harmony can thus be maintained.

Self-enquiry No.15: Sexuality

Sexuality is an area where most religions play a moralising role. They often reject pleasure, masturbation, homosexuality and sexual freedom. After centuries of moral conditioning, it may be difficult to face sexuality without embarrassment. No sexual behaviour should actually be condemned, as long as it is done out of free will with your partner and without causing any prejudice or harm.

If you have sexual taboos, what are they? What are you ashamed of? Return to the Source. Watch your thoughts: "I feel embarrassed", "I feel ashamed" or "I feel disturbed by" until they dissolve. You are now detached from your sexual "clouds" and consequently, they have no power over you.

Pure Consciousness includes all that is. When you integrate your sexual Being, you are not disturbed by any kind of sexual thoughts. "Clouds come and disappear". If you have desires that can be prejudicial to others, simply watch and accept them until they dissolve. Do not let such desires manifest into your life; but understand that they have the right to be in your mind and there are, definitely, many reasons why it is so. You are not responsible for it. Ego is only a "programme" in you. Do not identify with it and do not judge your mind. This way, it cannot control you.

What do you consider "bad", "unhealthy" or "abnormal": certain sexual behaviour, nudity, eccentric clothes, friendship between men and women in certain cultures? Return to the Source. Watch what you resist until all resistance ceases. Remain open-minded.

Understand well that as long as you reject something, it has an influence over your mind. For example, if it is forbidden to look at a beautiful rose, the mind dreams and thinks about it all the time. On the contrary, when the healthy mind sees a beautiful rose, beauty is simply seen and appreciated. The mind does not cling to it. In order for the mind not to cling to its desires, some people may have to open the "door of desires". This is a way to overcome them. However, at a certain point, this door has to be closed again in order to return to the Heart. Experience what you need to experience as respectfully as possible and then return to the Heart. Do not let desires lead you to weakness, disillusionment and selfishness. By experiencing what you needed to experience and by having the strength to free yourself from the mind, you find the real freedom of the Heart and realise the reality of true love.

The less you are conditioned by the concepts of "good" and "bad", the more your mind and behaviour are healthy. The mind is not trapped in the dynamics of attraction/repulsion. Sexuality is then natural. You are simply yourself and you let love and naturalness guide you.

Do you freely express your sexuality? If you cannot, what prevents you from relaxing and freely expressing your nature: fears, embarrassment, the "goal" or the need to prove? Welcome your "clouds" without resisting them and return to a place of inner relaxation. Let love and naturalness guide you.

Everybody is at a certain stage of sexual development. Every stage has to be respected, whether it is repressed, egoistical, provocative, rebellious or integrated. Welcome your ego as it is. It is the best way to transcend it.

The Third Gateway

Manipura Chakra
(level of the navel)
Self-esteem and Expression of Personal Potential

Self-enquiry No.16: Self-esteem and Identifications

Depending on how great your self-esteem is, you either express your potential or limit it.

If the lack of self-esteem prevents you from expressing your potential, open to your inner feeling of inferiority "I am not good enough", until it dissolves. Feel free to be yourself.

Observe how the fear or the feeling "I am not good enough" often comes from a lack of respect for your true nature. If you play a role that does not correspond to your true nature, you may not feel "well" or at ease. This is normal. Respect yourself. Do not feel obliged to do what makes you feel uncomfortable. See how, immediately, fears and the feeling of inferiority disappear. Also, do not let others force you into a role that is not yours. If the clouds "need to prove" or "fear of having to prove" cross your mind, watch them until they dissolve. Let decisions come from the Source. Follow your inner voice.

Observe also how some identifications may limit you. For example, if you are negatively identified with being a "bad painter" you may not be able to express your personal way of painting. If you like painting, let intuition guide you. If you identify with being a "Professor", you may not be able to receive the teaching of others. Don't we always have something to learn? Observe your clouds "negative identification" or "strict identification" until they dissolve.

When identification is strong, there may be comparison and worries. For example, if you identify strongly with being the bartender and people go next door to another bar, you may be affected. You may compare, compete and take what is happening in a personal way. Whatever you do in life, do your best and then surrender to existence.

If failure happens, it is also meaningful. There is always a reason for it. Sometimes it helps to let go of all that you cling to, to have more patience or to choose a direction that suits you better. In truth, there is no failure because it serves a purpose. You can even be grateful to the people who have participated in your failure because they are actually helping you to find your true expression.

Each identification is a limitation. It closes the personal field of expression. It may also limit the expression of others. For example, if you strictly identify with being a baker, you may think that learning piano is not for you. Similarly, the pianist may not get the chance to learn to make good bread. When identification is strong, there may be comparison and judgment. This can also be an impediment to personal development and respect for others.

> *How do you react according to your identification? If you are identified with the "strong" person, how do you judge the "weak"? If you are identified with the "pure", how do you judge the "impure"? What about the identification with the intelligent, educated or superior one? How do you judge the people you consider "inferior"? Observe each "strict identification" as a cloud in the sky of consciousness, until it dissolves. Return to a space of freedom and openness.*

Without judging people's roles and positions, we are free to be. Look at life as a play. *You are actually the only actor with different faces.* Now who do you think should be taken seriously? Simply be in harmony with your nature, whether it is artistic, intellectual, sporty, practical, contemplative, extrovert or introvert. Feel free to be who you are. Listen to your inner voice. Life can thus support you in the most optimal way to realise your true nature.

Self-enquiry No.17: Expression of Personal Potential

Here are a few more "clouds" that may prevent you from expressing your potential:

Do you like to control? Can you accept losing control? Return to the Source. Observe your cloud "need to control" until it dissolves. Trust other people.

Do you criticise others out of fear of being criticised yourself? How does this limit you? Return to the Source. Watch your cloud "need to criticise" until it dissolves. Maintain a space of mutual respect.

Are you over-confident? This may manifest as excessive joy. It may also result in a lack of sensitivity and openness. Do you see how over-confidence may also prevent you from opening to new experiences and opportunities that suit you better? Return to the Source. Watch your cloud "lack of openness" until it dissolves.

Do you often react against certain behaviour or words? If, in the past, you have suffered from being excessively controlled, you may run away from everything that seems to limit your freedom, independence or power to make decisions. These reactions may prevent you from finding your true area of expression. What makes you react? Return to the Source. Watch your cloud "reactive thought" until it dissolves. Let decisions come from a space of openness.

Do you worry about what other people think of you? Do you feel the need to conform? Do you feel the need to be recognised? Do you fear failure, taking risks or criticism?

Return to the Source. Observe your cloud "fear of other people's opinions" until it dissolves.

Self-enquiry No.18: Expression of Personal Potential

Fears are "normal" for someone who does not believe in the sacredness of life. They clearly vanish when confidence is there again. Whatever difficulties you go through, optimism and self-confidence always open doors. Do not let your shoulders hang, especially at the last milestone. Remember that the sun is ever present, even behind the thickest clouds. Find your inner silence and let your true nature express itself freely.

Your true nature may be ordinary. Can you accept it? Return to the Source and be yourself.

Your true nature may be special or extraordinary. Do you dare to reveal it? Return to the Source and express yourself freely.

Are you listening to your inner voice? What does it say? What are you interested in? What touches you? What motivates you? What makes you dream? Your inner nature definitely has something to express. It can be very simple, ordinary or extraordinary but still, it is present in the depth of yourself. Can you reconnect with your true nature in order to blossom and feel boundless joy?

When you follow your inner voice and do what corresponds to you, there is no need to compare. Inside, there is certainty. Even if others seem to do "better", this does not bother you because you do what is true to you. At this point, no external element can divert you from your path.

Can you go beyond the search for "better" and "perfect" to search for the expression of what is real for you? If you have the tendency to imitate others or to look for perfection, see what your fears are. Return to the Source and watch these fears until they dissolve.

Be yourself. Do not compare. There is a time for everything: a time to learn and a time to unlearn, a time to think of your own self and a time to think of others, a time for work and a time for leisure, a time to develop your potential and a time to express it. We are all part of the same house and we all play different roles. If everyone was an artist, we would be starving. If everyone painted the same painting, creation would be less flamboyant. Cooks are as necessary as salesmen and philosophers. May every cook express his/her own peculiarity. May all of us express our colours without worrying whether they are more or less beautiful than others. Whatever appearance you have (the coat you put on or the role you play), simply feel free. Is life not just a game where nothing should be taken too seriously, neither nakedness nor appearances? If today your expression is superficial, laugh about your mask! Similarly, if you manage to strip bare and be authentic, do not take your original face too seriously either!

Self-enquiry No.19: Personal Flowering

At any age, as long as you are happy and trusting, you are directly connected with your true nature and, therefore, you spontaneously know what you have to say or do. You are also directly connected with existence. Life can then show you the way. You are not alone. Divine love is in every form. Existence is your eternal Mother.

Do you believe in the sacredness of life? Can you do your best to be your true self and then trust existence to guide you towards your full bloom? If you cannot, return to the Source and watch your cloud "lack of trust" until it dissolves.

Can you recognise, accept and express your personal qualities? One day, a young girl stood up to dance in the middle of a chanting group. Some people thought she wanted to show off and criticised her. Isn't her behaviour beautiful though? She feels like dancing and she dances. She is also enjoying showing her dance. Is this not natural? This is what children often do. They show you their beautiful drawings, their dances, their beautiful poems and their new clothes.

This natural pride is sometimes so repressed that it transforms into hidden jealousy. If you suppress your true nature or your creativity, you may become jealous without even noticing it. Then, you tend to judge the people who dare to be themselves and express their talent, creativity and true nature. Remember who you truly are. Do not feel guilty. Welcome your clouds until they dissolve.

As long as your personal qualities are not recognised, there may be pride, jealousy, intolerance and even arrogance. Therefore, it is important to acknowledge your personal qualities.

See and welcome your personal qualities. Embrace also your divinity. Accept the fact that your true being is Love, Pure Consciousness. Let your true nature express itself freely.

Ego has absolutely no influence over you when both positive and negative qualities are recognised and accepted.

Self-enquiry No.20: Personal Flowering

Pride and vanity hide everywhere, even behind humble actions and apparently disinterested loving behaviour. Pride and vanity can also prevent personal flowering. The difference between an awakened person and someone still unconscious is that the awakened one knows his/her ego and vanity, while the other person is still unaware of it and resists it. The people who claim that ego does not exist should have a closer look to find where it is hiding so well. Ego plays tricks on people who do not want to face it.

Have you noticed your clouds of "pride" and "vanity"? Remember who you truly are. Return to the Source and observe these clouds until they dissolve.

What can you do when faced with vanity? The best thing is to laugh. Develop a good sense of humour! Actually, talking about humour, see if there are any jokes that disturb you.

Can you laugh about everything: yourself, your nationality and your religion? [21] *If you cannot laugh about yourself, what do you find disturbing about it? See and welcome the thought "I take myself too seriously". Do not feel "bad". Find the Source and see for yourself that you are "Nothing", a simple Presence.*

---

[21] As long as it is not disrespectful. Feel within you what the limit of respect is. Be sensitive to others.

Self-enquiry No.21: Personal Flowering

In general, individuals perceive the world and people in a very personal and subjective way because everybody has a different script in his/her mind. You can also call this script memories, conditioning, "wounds" or programming. People live in their world and tend to believe their world is right. This is the madness most individuals have. The mind is the instrument of this madness. It can justify thoughts and behaviour very well. Without awareness, you believe in your mental perception of reality, although it is false. Do you believe that madness has nothing to do with you? If so, allow me to help you have a closer look at your ego.

If you are afraid of what is not conventional, rational or "normal", you may be afraid of your hidden madness. Remember who you truly are. Return to the Source. Watch the cloud "fear of madness" until it dissolves.

Are your fears so strong that they distort reality (events, conversations and perception of people)? Yet, you strongly believe in your perception of reality and if someone would question it, this person would be the "mad one". Return to the Source. Watch your fears until they dissolve.

Do you have the tendency to see problems everywhere? Is your ego negative, distrustful, suspicious, easily accusative and sometimes paranoid? Know who you are. Return to the Source. See and accept the clouds "negativity", "fear" or "need to prove your worth" until they dissolve.

Is your perception of reality extremely selective? For example, you may pay attention to all the words or situations that seem to confirm your own views. Your beliefs seem very real even though they are false. Have you not noticed how a mind

*interested in red cars sees them all day long? In other words,
whenever you want to see certain things or certain people in a
certain way, you look for all the details that seem to confirm
your opinion. Remember who you truly are and return to the
Source. Welcome and accept your clouds "I need to prove I am
right" and "I feel insecure" until they dissolve. Observe how
your perception can be completely distorted and false.*

Everybody has more or less madness inside. It also hides behind
very smooth appearances. Again, the only difference between
someone awakened and someone still caught in illusion is that the
former knows there is a mad ego within everybody, while the latter
still denies it and often hides behind "normal" and "reassuring"
appearances. Really, all appearances are misleading! The recognition
of this madness is the first step towards a healthy mind. The person
who is still unaware tends to point his/her finger at the ones who make
mistakes. We all make mistakes at some point. However, when
madness is accepted inside, it loses its influence. It is also easier to
accept the madness in others as well as their mistakes. So, do not point
your finger at anyone, as we are all in the same boat.

The Fourth Gateway

Anahata Chakra
(level of the chest)
Faculty to Give and Receive Love

Self-enquiry No.22: Genuineness

On your way to Truth,
Some masks are hard to see and remove.
This is the mask of love, the mask of the good dove,
The mask of the pure, the mask of the saint, ever smooth.

So reassuring and flattering to wear,
They cover Truth, until you dare,
To see how ego can sometimes go,
Renouncing everything to look holy and ecstatic.

Mirror, is this a subtle game or truly authentic?
Moral conditioning is a delicate chain
To free yourself from and avoid being vain.

Fly bird, retrieve the hearth,
Of the unveiled, naked Heart,
The original Heart whose flight can now begin.

Love is who you truly are. You do not have to prove or force it. Some people wear very deceptive love masks but behind these masks, ego and suffering are hidden. Your heart does not have to be big. It simply has to be true and sincere. When you listen to your inner voice, love manifests as it needs to manifest (not always as you would like it to be).

If you have the tendency to play the loving person, return to the Source. See and accept your "love mask" until it dissolves. Let love express itself naturally through you.

Some people claim to love the whole world without realising that this love is an ego game. The "love ego" can also engage in

118

humanitarian projects or good deeds in an apparently disinterested way while it is just to prove its own value. This ego has all the appearance of love but the mind is in control. How can you recognise the "love ego"?

The "love ego" tends to compare and make other people feel guilty (in a subtle way or not) if they appear less "good" or less loving. Is this the case for you? Return to the Source. Observe your clouds until they dissolve.

Do you criticise or blame the people who do not give like you would expect them to give (of their time or hospitality, for example)? Do you blame the people who do not love as you think they should love? If so, return to the Source: a space of openness and acceptance of differences in the ways of being and loving. Watch your clouds until they dissolve.

Can you free yourself from being "good"? Do you dare to make decisions that you know are right but may lead to wrong judgments about yourself? Return to the Source and be yourself.

It is generally easier to play the role of the nice person and then to criticise. It is less easy to be authentic and to risk being considered the "bad" one. The free spirit is beyond good and bad. It does not belong to any side. Therefore, it is the supreme good. It preserves general harmony.

Sometimes your love is real but you don't really know how to love. This happens whenever you let your fears overcome your love (for your partner, child, friend, etc.).

What are your fears? Do they manifest as excessive and accusative criticisms? Are they really legitimate? Can you manage to keep an open dialogue and relationship? Do you give the other person the right to act and think differently than

119

you? Can you let go of your need to protect and control? Return to the Source. Observe your clouds until they dissolve. Let love express itself freely.

Finally, what is your love for the Divine like? Many so-called devotees or spiritual people bow down before their God or Master while continuing to judge, be intolerant and lie.

Is your love for God truly sincere or out of self-interest? Return to the Source and open to truth.

Self-enquiry No.23: Love Relationships

As long as the truth about your ego is not understood, you look for and meet the alter-ego, whether as a friend or as a lover. These types of relationships are actually your best teachers to reveal what you resist. However, when you make peace with your inner ego, the outer ego does not have a negative influence on you. It transforms into a soul mate.

What is your relationship like? Is your relationship true? Is it flowing? A real relationship is open to truth and each partner is willing to "grow together". Do you love with your mind or with your heart? When love comes from the heart, you can accept your partner's imperfections. On the other hand, when love comes from the mind, there is no desire to accept the partner's defects. If you are confused and lack clarity, return to the Source. Let inner silence and life guide you.

Love from the mind is a cause of disillusionment because it is superficial. For example, if you try to be liked without really being yourself, the greater your chance of disappointment is. By playing a certain game, you attract the people sensitive to that game. Inevitably, one day, you get trapped by your own scenario. The partner may just love the image you want to show and not the real you. Authenticity is the key to healthy relationships which can cope with life's difficulties and allow mutual growth. The mature companion is the sincere friend who cares for you. It is the friend you like, of course, but whose imperfections you can accept. It is the friend you feel perfectly at ease with, the one you can talk to about everything and be bare without any embarrassment.

Do you enjoy your partner's presence? Do you accept his/her imperfections? Can you be real and without any mask? If not, return to the Source and be yourself. By being your true self, clarity automatically comes. Let this clarity guide you.

Do you feel somehow uncomfortable with your partner? Do you play a game? Do you try to "possess" your partner by ruse, games or strategies? Do you believe jealousy is a proof of love? What fears prevent you from really being yourself? Return to the Source and watch your fears until they dissolve. Let your true nature flow freely.

The truer you are, the fewer disappointments there are. You also know more quickly if your relationship can be harmonious.

Self-enquiry No.24: Love Relationships

There can be peace and harmony in a relationship when partners have common values and a similar understanding of what a relationship is.

What do you expect from a relationship (sharing, family, pleasure, freedom)? The goals may vary from one partner to the other. For some people, the priority is freedom. For others, it is the family. When priorities are different, are you willing to accept your differences and make the necessary concessions? When the cloud "refusal of concessions" crosses your mind, watch it until it dissolves.

Can you communicate freely about everything? If so, the relationship is healthy and can evolve, even if values are different. When the cloud "refusal of communication" is in your mind, watch it until it dissolves.

Do you believe that peace is the ultimate goal of a relationship? Is it the destination that counts or the way the couple walks on the path? Very rare are the couples who always live peacefully. But happy are the couples who have understood that true peace is a way to welcome and resolve the difficulties that may occur in life.

Can you welcome potential difficulties as a way to open to a deeper love? When your mind refuses the idea of difficulties, return to the Source. Watch your cloud "refusal of difficulties" until it dissolves. Go with the flow. Surrender.

A relationship goes through different phases. There may even come a time when one of the partners feels a need for change. What can we think about change? Every couple walks together along a sort of circle (a cycle). The partners first fall in love. They often believe they have found the ideal partner. Then, they start experiencing the first difficulties related to their respective personalities. They may, or may not, deal with these difficulties very well. They may even manage to live peacefully but then, the absence of problems may become a problem. Peace may seem boring. The feeling of being in love as in the first days is no more there. In addition, each partner has to cope with the routine of daily life. How can they maintain a beautiful relationship? As the couple reaches the end of the circle, a "crisis" may come. Will one of them choose to end the relationship? If so, what happens? They start again another cycle with a different partner and may face the same difficulties until they have finally had enough experiences or are mature enough to make the "leap" into love. Why doesn't this leap happen easily? Real love is not attractive to the ego. It is the end of all illusions and "ideals". Yet, do not be afraid of the real flavour of love. When ego is conquered, there is true joy and love. Make the leap. With clarity, false "dreams" and illusions vanish. Then, you are really free. You are not free to do whatever your ego wants or desires. You are free to open to real love and to be Love. Relationships are also a sacred path to the Divine.

Are you ready for love? Can you accept the ups and downs of a relationship? Can you forget the past and forgive each other for your mistakes? Can you try to overcome your respective limitations? Can you help and support each other through that? Do you really wish this?

A relationship evolves and may even sometimes reach the stage of incompatibility and saturation but this can change too. Can you try your best to maintain harmony with your partner and the rest of the family (especially if you have children)? When you go through difficult times, keep in mind that the happiest people do not necessarily have the "best". They simply appreciate what they have." [22]

---

[22] Warren Buffet.

Be patient. Everybody changes. Look for solutions. Nourish your inner joy. Separate temporarily if it is necessary. Do your best and at the same time, let go of expectations. Surrender. What has to happen will happen. Do not worry. Relax. Simply do what feels natural. Let the mystery of life unravel. One fine day, the solution clearly appears.

In some cases, differences are too great for there to be a true relationship. Then, it seems preferable to separate amicably and to maintain, in this way, a harmonious relationship. What are the obstacles to this type of separation?

Do you persist in accepting a situation that does not correspond to you at all? What is the reason for your attachment? Open to truth. See what your fears are. Find your inner silence and your freedom.

Do you try to tie your partner up with a rope out of fear s/he will escape? This is actually real loss. What is real cannot die. What is untrue can only last at the cost of disillusionment and suffering. If you try to keep a relationship alive by force, tricks, jealousy or calculation, don't you create bondage for yourself? If this is the case, understand the reason for your attachment and meet your fears inside. Free yourself.

Self-enquiry No.25: Love Relationships

If your relationship is difficult and complex, I invite you to see the situation more clearly by answering the questions below.

What does each partner think about the relationship? What are the difficulties generated by your partner? What are the difficulties generated by yourself?

How do you try to improve your relationship (discussions, criticisms, blame)? What did this bring so far? Can there be other ways to improve your relationship (communicate differently, give each other more space or turn to an outside counsellor)?

Is it possible to totally accept your partner the way s/he is today? Can you stop trying to change your partner? For that, clearly consider what you blame her/him for. See whether you have the willingness or strength to accept without complaining what you consider to be her/his imperfections.

With clarity, solutions unfold. The Heart finds the most appropriate solution to preserve harmony.

Self-enquiry No.26: Giving

When fears do not bind your true nature, giving is a very natural movement. This movement happens according to the sense of harmony. For example, if your personal financial situation is satisfactory, giving is very natural. On the other hand, if you do not have a lot of money and you need to take care of your family, giving is no longer natural. Giving depends on the personal situation and circumstances. It does not obey moral obligations.

If giving is not natural for you, return to the Source. Watch your fears until they dissolve.

Again, remember that you are truly not the ego. So simply dare to face it. Open to truth. Otherwise, you may believe that you are already free when you are still the puppet of your mental conditioning. Some ego tendencies may remain "hidden", especially with regard to giving and receiving. So really free yourself from your ego programme by opening to truth. For example, when you have fears that prevent you from giving, do you find excuses to justify your behaviour? What are they? Open to truth in order to really respect other people and yourself. When you open to truth, egoic behaviour naturally disappears.

Do you have selfish excuses (e.g. "I will not start helping these people otherwise they will take all that I have")? If so, return to the Source and watch your cloud until it dissolves. Be trusting.

Do you have accusative excuses ("I will not buy them a nice present because they are stingy")? Often, the stingy person tends to accuse others of stinginess just as the liar tends to accuse others of lying. Return to the Source and watch your cloud until it dissolves. Be true with yourself and others.

Do you have blaming excuses ("I can take this bathrobe from the hotel because they charge such high rates for the rooms")? If so, return to the Source. Watch your cloud until it dissolves. Be respectful.

Do you have the "victim excuses" ("They do not care much about me, so I don't see why I should care about them.")? Do you expect a lot from others while on the other hand you give very little? If so, return to the Source. Watch your cloud until it dissolves. Open your mind and enjoy the satisfaction sharing brings.

The mind may criticise others in order to free itself from guilt. Do you recognise yourself in this role? If so, return to the Source. Welcome your cloud "cunningness" (it is never your fault but other people's fault) until it dissolves.

Open also to truth in regard to your way of giving. Who is the giver: the ego or the Heart?

Do you give out of self-interest (e.g. to use people's services or to keep up a good reputation)? Do you give differently depending on the importance and position of the people you are with? Return to the Source. See what your fear is. Watch it until it dissolves.

Do you give out of moral obligations? Do you force yourself to give your time, attention or money? Return to the Source. Watch your fear until it dissolves.

Why force love when at the core of your being you have never ceased being love? True love cannot be forced. However, there are differences in the way some people force themselves to do good. Some may want to help others only out of self-interest (e.g. to improve their own karma).[23] This is useless because the motivation is selfish. On the other hand, some people genuinely want to overcome their selfish habits and they do their best to be "good". This is very virtuous behaviour. The sincerity of intentions is what really matters. Authenticity is the source of happiness. Every action and thought coming from this source is "pure" (true). It brings harmony. Even anger coming from this source is not destructive. Do not be afraid of giving, even if what you give is not recognised. Know that what you give out of sincerity is a precious gift, for others, and also for you.

Open yourself to the thought "I give without expecting anything in return". Return to the Source. If the fact of giving without receiving anything in return disturbs you, watch your clouds "frustration" or "anger" until they dissolve.

The more you give out of sincerity, the more life rewards you in one way or another, sooner or later, directly or indirectly. Life has millions of hands and millions of ways to thank you. Yet, do not expect anything in return. Simply let love express itself freely through you.

---

[23] Law of cause and effect. Consequences of previous actions.

Self-enquiry No.27: Receiving

Giving and receiving are very natural movements. However, depending on each person's history, giving love may not always be easy. So is the case with receiving love. What about you? You may find it difficult to receive love and help from others when you feel it is not sincere. Otherwise, what prevents you from opening to love?

Is it pride? Is it the habit of dealing with everything alone? Is it too many disappointments which make you believe that true love does not exist? Is it guilt, the belief that you are not good enough to deserve help and love? Return to the Source. Watch your mind until clouds dissolve. Welcome love.

Do you fear misjudgement if you cannot give in return? Return to the Source and watch your fear until it dissolves. When giving in return is not possible, don't you think that life has hands other than yours to thank someone? Your sincere intention to give in return will definitely find a way to express itself, even if it is not directly through your own self. Let love manifest freely.

Self-enquiry No.28: Receiving

Lack of self-love is the basic reason why some people refrain from giving and receiving love. Sometimes, this lack of self-love makes a person behave in a mean way, as if to really prove that s/he is a "bad" person. Is this the case for you?

Do you sometimes behave in a mean way? Can you reconcile with your inner "demon" (the hard-hearted, selfish, jealous, domineering one)? Remember who you truly are. Do not identify with ego. Return to the Source and observe your clouds in a detached way until they dissolve. Remain open.

In daily life, each time "mean thoughts" pass through your mind, be conscious of them without judging them, until they dissolve. Then, they have no power over you. How wonderful!

You may hide your inner demon. The people who have a hidden demon generally know how to control themselves and they like to control. They can also wear a gentle mask. However, when the "control" is lost, they may become aggressive or mean (even in subtle ways). Can you recognise your hidden demon? Can you reconcile with it? Do not identify with ego. Do not feel "bad". Return to the Source and see what your inner demon is. Watch it until it dissolves.

All demons exist within each of us. You are not your body but Consciousness that includes all bodies. The only difference between people is that some are already reconciled with their demons and others are not. Do not point your finger at the demons in others because that would just be mocking your own self. By not resisting the truth, you neutralise all "demons".

Some people cannot open to love because they are used to functioning with a "stick". If you treat them nicely, they may not be able to open to your gentleness and respect it because the relational mode they know is constraint and force.

If you lack respect for gentle people because you judge them as weak or hypocritical, see your "doubt" and clouds. Are you too hard with yourself? Return to the Source and watch your clouds until they dissolve. Welcome gentleness.

Love cannot be understood by the mind. It seems too naïve and unintelligent. Take as an example the behaviour of pet dogs. Even if you correct them, they still wag their tail the next moment.

Do you love Love? Can you really open to it? Love knocks at your door but does not impose itself. So the opening has to come from both sides.

Do you fear love? Are you afraid of suffering if you are trusting, innocent and vulnerable? Return to the Source. Watch your fear until it dissolves. Let love be.

It may seem easier to be protective, calculating, clever or manipulative. You may mistakenly think this protects you from suffering. Believe in the sacredness of existence. Wherever you are, you are in Mother's arms. Open to life and to love.

The Fifth Gateway

Vishuddhi Chakra
(throat)
Communication and Creativity

Self-enquiry No.29: Free Expression

People's natures and gifts are different. Some are gifted towards manual work, some others, intellectual activities, verbal expression, healing, painting, dancing, singing or simply relaxing and enjoying life.

What are your talents or natural inclinations? Can you welcome them and express them freely?

When you forget about yourself, your true nature is free. Activities happen naturally. Actions unfold. The brush paints. The pen reveals the meaning. The hands heal. Dance happens. The voice sings. The clown makes funny faces but the actor has vanished. The eyes simply delight in the surroundings. Truth expresses itself. Free expression is a state of Presence. It is your natural state.

If you are afraid of expressing yourself freely, what prevents you from doing so? What are your fears: "I fear people's judgments", "I am afraid of making mistakes", "I do not feel qualified enough", "I would seem too superficial", "I would ridicule myself" "I am afraid of saying uninteresting things"? Return to the Source. Watch your fears until they dissolve.

Do you easily criticise the people who express themselves freely? What does this hide? Do you accept your own weaknesses? Return to the Source. Observe your inner clouds until they dissolve.

Self-enquiry No.30: Lies and Truth

People who have been severely scolded in their childhood for their mistakes generally prefer to lie rather than tell the truth. If you ask children what mistakes they made, they tell you. However, if you scold them afterwards, they may end up telling lies. This may continue in adult life. This is why certain people cannot face situations where they have to admit their faults, tell the truth or face criticism.

Do you often lie? Can you accept the liar in you? Do you have the tendency to believe other people lie to you? Do you accuse others instead of facing the consequences of your acts? If so, return to the Source. Watch your clouds until they dissolve.

Even if your lies are insignificant, why would you prefer them to truth? Do you really believe that small lies and excuses simplify situations? Why wouldn't the truth be better accepted than a lie? It can be told with sensitivity. For example, if you are tired and do not feel like visiting some friends, you can tell them the truth in a simple and gentle way. You should also be capable of hearing the truth.

Can you easily hear the truth? Can you accept the fact that some people do not appreciate you or do not want to see you? When the thought "I cannot accept this" crosses your mind, return to the Source. Welcome your resistance until it dissolves.

Of course, there are situations when silence or even a "nice lie" is preferable to truth, but otherwise, what would prevent you from telling or hearing the truth?

Do you easily feel rejected? Are you still identified with the "bad" person? Each time thoughts like "I am a bad person", "I am afraid of people's judgments" or "I am afraid of being rejected" cross your mind, return to the Source. Welcome your clouds until they dissolve.

Self-enquiry No.31: Lies and Truth

In my opinion, expressing feelings and even anger is better than being quiet. This way, you do not carry a "weight" in your heart and there is room for "growing together". Otherwise, by not expressing yourself, your heart may close. You may become cold, taciturn, frustrated or hypocritical.

If you don't freely express what you think or feel, welcome inwardly the feeling of frustration, indifference or your hypocrisy (gossiping or criticising behind people's backs). Return to the Source. Do not identify with ego. Do not feel guilty. Open to truth and watch your clouds until they dissolve.

On the contrary, you may express yourself very freely to the extent of being misunderstood or misjudged. If, for example, you can laugh about your ego, it is easy for you to strip bare. However, if the person in front of you has not "digested" his/her own ego tendencies, this openness may be misunderstood. In some cases, it is preferable to wear a veil of silence over your mind. By avoiding exposing certain aspects of the ego, harmony is maintained.

If you talk too openly, can you accept being naive or lacking discernment? Return to the Source and watch your clouds until they dissolve. Feel what can be said depending on the individuals. Trust your inner voice.

Finally, how do you express your opinions and assert yourself? Who is in command of your expression: the ego or the Heart?

Are you arrogant? Do you have the tendency to believe you know better than others, especially when you are with people you consider weaker, inferior or more ignorant than you?

Return to the Source. Do not identify with ego. Open to your arrogance until it dissolves.

Are you weak? If people freely assert their point of view and you do not feel comfortable to talk to them, do you accuse them (or feel like accusing them) of being the arrogant ones? Return to the Source. Observe your clouds "weakness" or "lack of courage" until they dissolve. What are the consequences of your weakness? Do you criticise or gossip too much? Return to the Source. Do not identify with ego. Watch your clouds until they dissolve.

Arrogance and weakness often lead to vain conversations. When you are "trapped" in this kind of conversation and the person whom you are speaking to is not open, calmly and clearly assert your point of view and then stop talking. Even if you are right, accept being the "loser". Truly, there are no losers in the "game" of life.

After Crossing the Forest of Shadows

Finally, your mind is at peace. You have explored, understood and accepted the different aspects of your ego. This inner peace is now your true pillar. The outer reality does not affect you as it did before. If some people have wrong opinions about you, it does not disturb you. You know your own truth and you can welcome your shadows. Therefore, you are like a tree that is both deeply rooted in the soil and can also dance in the wind. It is a beautiful scene.

After going through all these pages, you may have a certain idea of the person you should be. If so, rid yourself right away of any "idea" of a model. Especially, do not evaluate yourself or other people on a spiritual scale (level of joy, level of fears, level of energy, level of silence and level of love). Otherwise, you would fall into the major trap: judgment and the search for a self that is anything other than you are right now, in the present moment. Take everything lightly. Free yourself from spiritual ideals, perfection, other people's expectations and guilt. Simply be yourself and do your best. Do not try to be exceptional, different or special. Accept your ego as it is, "here and now".

Keep observing your clouds in daily life, and in particular the four main ones: "expectations", "need to prove your worth", "need to blame and criticise" and "fear of losing". Remember them. Be conscious of them when they cross your mind. Know who you truly are and maintain your openness.

There is nothing exceptional, brilliant, powerful or perfect to search for. You are simply a part of nature. Is there anything simpler than nature? Some trees are big and some trees are small. Some plants are robust and others frail. Some bushes have thorns and others don't. Each element is where it has to be. There is no comparison. There is no judgment. Everything functions as a whole entity, in harmony. You are now part of this harmony because your heart guides you. Let your

139

true nature express itself freely. Do what is simple, natural, self-evident and harmonious.

Meanwhile, do not even let the subtle ego trap you. Do not deny ego or think it is no longer there or should no longer be there. You have simply stepped out of it by being aware of it. Ego is not a problem. Keep seeing it, welcome it and laugh about it. With awareness, it disappears without effort. For the friend of Light and shadows, there is no duality. Everything is welcome. The mind is no longer trapped and limited.

Chapter 6: Be Your Natural Self

Marie, 4 years old.

About Happiness

When the inner conflict ceases, duality comes to an end. You are natural and you can listen to your heart. However, the ego may reappear from time to time on the screen of consciousness. So keep being vigilant in order to remain free and natural. A few other keys can help you.

There is a traditional story about a king who could not decide to which one of his three sons he would hand over the golden key to his kingdom. One day, he announced that he would give this key to the son who would be completely happy after ten years. Nothing appeared to be easier to the three sons. They had always been very happy and blessed with easy lives, money and the best counsellors.

The first son thought he would conquer the heart of the most beautiful and intelligent princess. When he would inherit her kingdom, he would become the happiest and most admired son. Ten years later the prince succeeded. He was admired and respected by all. All the people in the kingdom regarded him as a model of success. After ten years his father asked him whether he felt happy. The question seemed out of place to the son. Why wouldn't he be happy? He had everything he needed to be happy. "Are you sure about it?" his father asked. It was true that in spite of his beautiful princess and the admiration he received, he sometimes felt lonely. He was missing someone to laugh and feel completely at ease with. But if his beautiful princess were to give him a son, he would be the happiest of all men. "Your happiness is always conditional" answered his father. "Can you build true happiness on 'ifs' and 'hopes'? Can happiness be dependent upon success? What's more, the other day I met an old man who told me that you so badly wanted to believe in your own happiness that you could not easily question yourself. Is this true my son?"

The second son thought he would find perfect happiness by following the precepts of the sages. A first sage advised him to do a retreat and keep silent for seven years. He did this and the experience made him very wise. Still, he did not feel completely happy. A second

143

counsellor blamed him for having listened to the first sage and advised him not to have any negative thoughts for a whole year. So he did not and he became wiser, but still, he did not find true happiness. A third sage advised him to have some fun. Also, this did not bring the expected satisfaction. In the ninth year, the son read a lot of wise books. He met lots of learned men and, of course, he followed their precepts. In the tenth year, his father asked him whether he had found true happiness. "I am a lot wiser than before but I have to admit that I have not really found happiness. Deep down, I even feel a little depressed" answered the son. The father then asked: "Isn't this because you follow and listen to others? But what do *you* really want, my son, in your life? Do you listen to yourself? Do you know what is right and real for you? Do you know what desires and fears prevent you from doing what you like and from really being yourself?"

It is easy to guess that the third son inherited the golden key to the kingdom. From the very beginning he laughed at the idea of being totally and always happy. As if this was possible! Curious to see what would be behind the mountains, he left. He met a large number of people, followed the advice that seemed wise to him and ignored the recommendations he did not like. He became a navigator when he felt like it, a gardener when this appealed to him, a road sweeper when he was broke and a writer when he had some money. He lived lightly but still had projects and ideas in his mind. When his projects and ideas were realised, so much the better. When they were not, he did not mind. Nothing was too important. Still, he considered everything as precious. His father asked him whether he was happy. "I have no idea", he answered. "What is happiness? In any case, I am satisfied with my life the way it is today with its ups and downs. I don't regret anything about my past and I don't worry about the future. My heart is light. Maybe it is so because I have been listening to myself."

The second son also had all the qualities to find this simple happiness but he was not listening enough to his inner voice. In the same way, some spiritual seekers are so much in search of liberation that they forget the *heart* of the "problem": to simply be themselves and follow their natural inclinations. How could you open to your true self if you don't respect who you are? How can you be happy if you don't even know what it means to have self-respect and to really be yourself?

I shall tell you another story. A little girl spent most of her time looking at butterflies. When people asked her what she wanted to do later in life, she always answered: "Draw butterflies". This made her whole family laugh. But when she grew up and her answer remained the same, her parents thought it was time to show her "the right path": have a good job, be independent, make a good living and thus be happy. But when she turned eighteen, the girl's answer remained the same: "I want to draw butterflies". "How can you make a living by drawing butterflies?" asked her parents. They forced her to study accountancy and she became an accountant. At the age of thirty, she felt depressed. Her whole life seemed uninteresting. Was this the happiness her parents had planned for her? She spoke to her friends about her idea to draw butterflies but they told her it was unreasonable. She would risk making her depression worse if she failed. She had to be wiser, more responsible and accept working and living like everybody else. In the end, like everybody else, she would learn to be satisfied with what she had. So she tried to be satisfied with her situation. At the age of forty, she felt even more depressed. This made her seriously consider what had become of her life. She was not running her life. Her life was run by the voices of her parents, the voices of her friends and the voices of society. What were all these voices? Fears, only fears, more and more fears. Fortunately, she finally decided to listen to her inner voice and she found true happiness.

When some ideas sound right within, they cannot be false in life. If you have confidence in what you feel deep within, it is impossible to fail. Of course, your project should not just be a fleeting or superficial idea, motivated by ambition or the need to prove something. It has to be true and natural. If so, and when possible, just be courageous and take the leap into truth. Believe in yourself. Your inner force will hold you by all means and by all its strength. Be patient and believe in your inner dream. It will come true.

Follow Your Intuition and Be Happy

When there is no inner conflict, ego does not obstruct the way. You are in direct contact with your true nature and consequently, you have intuition. You also receive help from existence.

Can you let intuition guide you? Can you put aside your rational mind? What is the truth of your heart? Welcome it. What do you feel within? Trust your natural response.

However difficult some situations may be, when you are in tune with yourself, your joy is not troubled. This inner joy (or inner confidence) is your greatest strength. Whatever you have to face in life, it supports you. It heals all your wounds. It helps you quickly recover from difficulties. You can never be "down" for a long time. It makes you quickly forget about the past and live in the present moment. So nurture your inner joy because this is what gives you real strength. Follow your intuition.

Generally, we can say that people walking on the outer path (open to life experiences) feel more joyous and balanced when they also nourish their inner silence (by walking in nature, staying alone for some time, practicing yoga, meditation, etc.). On the other hand, people walking on the inner path (spiritual practices, meditation, retreats) can nourish their inner joy by opening to the outer world (having a drink somewhere or chatting with friends). When the opening is balanced, there is great stability and true joy.

Be Happy: Everything is Alright Anyway

Sometimes, choices have to be made and clarity is not always present. When you have doubts or are afraid of making a wrong choice, return to your inner silence. Can this silence be affected? It cannot. So, what is there to be afraid of? Feel free to make mistakes. This is actually the best way to avoid them. You remain spontaneous. In any case, making mistakes is a way to learn and grow. Everything is alright anyway. It is only when the mind interferes that life appears complicated. The lack of clarity is not a problem. It simply means that the time for clarity has not yet come. So, take everything lightly and know that it is all relative. Return to your inner silence. Do not worry. When the time to make a decision really comes, you know it. All is clear. Relax. Be light-hearted and joyful!

Happiness and Freedom

Sometimes you may be confused. Who is ruling your life? Is it the Heart (sensitive to general harmony)? Is it the inner wisdom (beyond good and evil) or is it the mind (fed by ambition, fears, morality, anger, guilt and the need to compare)? Observe your inner feelings. Truth simply unveils. Here is an example. Several years ago, I wanted to teach Yoga but I also had the desire to look for a social or humanitarian work. But who wanted this? When I observed my inner feelings, the answer was clear. For Yoga my whole being said "yes". On the contrary, any other projects felt heavy inside. Without being aware of this, I would have thrown myself into activities that were against my natural inclinations. I would have forced myself.

Simply feel within yourself how certain ideas or projects resonate. Do they feel light, heavy, pleasant or unpleasant? Trust your natural response. Beyond the sense of duty and morality, act according to your inner voice. It always brings harmony, not only for you but also for others. Ultimately, if we all respect this inner voice, it will lead us to global harmony. Do not be influenced by your mind, other people's minds or various familial and social pressures. Trust yourself and be free. Trust is the key to your happiness.

Two beautiful leaves whirled around,
In love with freedom's silent sound.
Longing to see the ocean they whispered to the wind
"Free us from this endless whirl".

One day, a sun bird flew around
And slipped a message in the winds.
"If you want to see the ocean, darling leaves
Follow the stream and drop the mind.
Do not wish for anything else and have no fears,
Soon you will see the ocean."

The first leaf landed on the stream,
Without fear and without resisting.
She followed the current until she almost drowned
But each time got pulled up and found
Mildest waters to curl around.
.
One morning after drying its dew,
The leaf saw the ocean, how blue!
Flooded with love,
It bathed in the delightful abode!

The second leaf, a cleverer one,
Followed the first whirlpool to the bank.
Why undergo these wild waters? To be frank,
The scene is softer around!
The leaf took its time and found,
That nothing matters but having fun – Why be profound?

Proud to be thoughtful and to avoid danger,
It followed the stream as it pleased. Is this surrender?
Oh dear leaf, now you understand,
That the freedom of the mind is not the freedom of the Heart.

This is the paradox of freedom. When you think you are free because you do whatever you want, you are actually alienated. On the contrary, when you give up your own will and listen to your heart, you move towards the greatest freedom: being truly yourself. Are you ready to let go of the mind control? Have a look at it. What is your apparent freedom? What are your choices? What is your will-power? What is leading your life? As you know, almost all your choices are conditioned by desires, fears, morality, expectations, education and experiences. You believe yourself to be free whereas you are entangled in a web of conditioning. Prisoner of this web, your freedom is to be aware of where your desires come from. This is the beginning of freedom and its paradox: finding freedom in renouncing your will-power. It is no longer "I want" that leads you but "I feel" which expresses your true nature: the Heart. See the difference: "I want to have fun now" and "I feel it is better to take care of the children beforehand". "I want" is self-centred and "I feel" brings harmony. Surrender to this greater intelligence. Go with its flow. It inevitably runs to the Ocean, whether the water gets rough or not. *Trust* is the key word.

Happiness and the Respect for General Harmony

Is your life natural or controlled by ego? You are natural when you respect general harmony (respect for yourself as well as for other human beings, animals and nature as a whole). All forms being your real body, it does not make sense to disrespect them. The question of respect sets the limit between ego and non-ego. What is natural (respectful) directly comes from the Heart. What is disrespectful comes from the ego. This gives you clarity. You know if ego influences you or not.

Observe animals. Generally, they do not hunt for their mere pleasure. They hunt when hungry or to feed their babies. Hence, the natural order is respected and preserved. Ego is absent. In the same way, you are natural (without ego) when you are sensitive to general harmony. In all of us and in different ways, our inner voice knows what is natural and harmonious. No rules are needed when we are sensitive and conscious. We are naturally respectful.

In order to know whether your behaviour is natural (without ego) or not, ask yourself the following question: "Am I respectful?" What does your inner voice tell you? For example, "Am I respectful when I lie?" Well, obviously, it all depends on the lie and on circumstances. A lie is natural when it protects somebody. It is not natural if it protects selfish interests. If you are honest with yourself, you know the answer. But do not fall into the trap of ego justifications. The mind can certainly find hundreds of convincing excuses to avoid facing the truth. Face the inner truth with courage and honesty. Like this, personal answers can be found to any types of questions:

Is it natural not to care about ecology and the quality of the goods we buy? Is it natural to pollute our planet? Is it natural to treat animals in a bad way? Is it natural to kill mosquitoes? Is it natural to hunt? Is it natural to eat a lot of meat? Is it natural to be angry? Is it natural to make a vow of celibacy? Is it natural to have several partners? Is it natural to treat women differently from men? Is it natural to have an abortion? Is it natural to be very active? Is it natural to do nothing? Is it natural to ask for a lot of money in exchange for services? Is it natural not to ask for money for your work? What does your inner voice tell you?

All answers depend upon individuals and circumstances. There cannot be any fixed general rules. Whatever decision you make, it has to be conscious. *You have to be truly at peace with your mind.* In this way, you can come out of the mind box and traditional morality. In the past, judgment ("good and bad") and also the refusal of judgment ("It is not good to judge") have often prevented humanity from being free, respectful and from evolving harmoniously.

Are you free and respectful? Do you do your best to respect yourself, others and nature in general? Do you equally do your best to trust and respect the choices and decisions of others?

To be happy, let us be free and respectful.

Happiness and Lightness of Mind

The mind is very demanding sometimes. When your head becomes too heavy, bring your attention elsewhere. Look around. Listen to the bird's song. Hear the traffic passing by. Feel the sensation of the wind on your skin. Observe your inner feelings. Observe the beauty of your surroundings or the shape of the buildings around you. Like this, in a split-second you can stop being trapped by your mind. You return to your inner silence and to the Heart. Being rooted in the Heart brings joy and harmony. It is the inner spring that nurtures all things. So, take everything lightly and be happy!

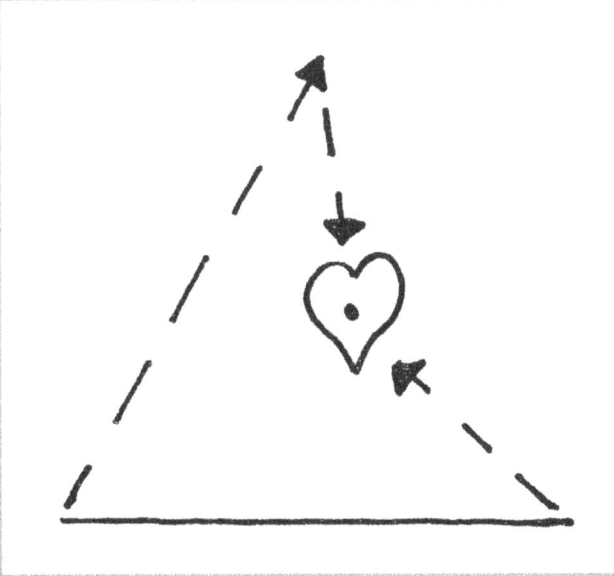

What is Enlightenment?

For a long time, I doubted my experience because it did not resemble the extraordinary stories of the enlightened sages I had heard about. However, I could see that Pure Consciousness can only be met in no-time, "now", because time belongs to the mind. When the mind forgets itself, time does not exist. Only Truth *is*.

A book finally helped me to end my doubts about the meaning of enlightenment or illumination. It says: "When the object is identical with the light of consciousness, it is Grace[24]." "Pure I-consciousness is not of a relational type. It and the universe are One. It is immediate awareness. When one has this consciousness, one knows one's true nature. This is what is meant by liberation". [25] Nonetheless, can we truly speak about liberation if most of us are trapped by illusion? True liberation is the reconciliation of every branch of the tree. Is this not the real meaning and mystery of life: the awakening of the whole tree so that we can live our existential adventure freely and joyously? When beings are free, they directly manifest the truth of their hearts.

The Different Paths to Enlightenment

According to the same book,[26] there are two paths to realise the Self: the direct and the progressive way. They can also be called respectively "the outer path" and "the inner path" (see drawing).[27] The inner path (progressive way) is the path of the seeker who searches for

---

[24]Jaideva Singh, *The Secret of Self-Recognition*, Motilal Banarsidass publishers, private limited, Delhi, p.38.
[25] Jaideva Singh, ibid., pp. 27-31.
[26] Jaideva Singh, Ibid., p.38.
[27] The left "arrow" represents the inner path (progressive way) and the right "arrow" represents the outer path (direct way).

awakening through techniques: meditation, energy work and specific practices. The process of enlightenment is progressive because the mind goes through different states of consciousness[28] before reaching the point of the Heart. *If these experiences are not taken too seriously (whether they are extraordinary, blissful or frightening)*, the mind can detach from them and realise its true nature.

The process of awakening can also be direct (outer path). Through life experiences, the individual has naturally reconciled with the different aspects of the ego. There is no duality. Therefore, the mind does not go through different states of consciousness. It transcends them all directly when the point of the Heart is reached. This is the experience of illumination. On this path, the Heart is the guide. When the time for enlightenment has come, the Heart calls you: "Wake up!" If you listen to this call, you can effortlessly and instantly realise your true nature. There is no other experience. With the spark of an intense longing for truth, direct opening is possible. Speak the truth, seek truth, open to truth, have an immense love for truth and you will find it.

---

[28] "This is the way to Samadhi (contemplation, mental absorption). It may lead to the state of Turya, before knowing the state of Turiyatita. Normally, human consciousness only functions in three states: the waking state, the dream state and deep sleep. In the state of Turya, consciousness is detached and aware of all the three states. It is not under the influence of maya, which brings about a sense of difference. In this state, manas (the sensory aspects of the mind) becomes attenuated but not yet dissolved in Shakti (the energy of the universe) as is the case in the state of turyatita. When the state of turya is completely developed and has reached perfection, it is transformed into turyatita which transcends everything." Jaideva Singh, ibid., p.146.

Conditions for Enlightenment

The realisation of your true nature requires the opening of the sixth[29] and seventh chakras.[30] For this, three main conditions are required: inner peace, Self-knowledge and a state of Presence. When these conditions are fulfiled, enlightenment happens. The previous chapters have established the foundations to realising your true nature: Self-knowledge and inner reconciliation. The following pages help you to lift the last veils, so that the state of Presence (steady openness) manifests effortlessly.

The point of the Heart is your destination. It is the point zero that transcends time (the mind). It is the point of balance and non-duality. "The Heart is the deepest consciousness. It is the centre of reality. It is the light of consciousness in which the whole universe is rooted."[31] The opening to the Heart happens in a state of total acceptance of the ego: the state of non-resistance.[32] It is a state of perfect openness. Direct awakening happens when you are *sensitive to general harmony, open to the truth about your ego, aware of your true nature and totally absorbed in what you are doing.* Be totally one-pointed, passionate, intense or totally silent. While dancing, singing, making love, reading, painting, doing sports, meditation or any daily tasks, be present, "One" with what you are doing. Do not think. Meeting the present moment and therefore the Self is totally unexpected.

If the moment of enlightenment has not yet come, do not worry. What truly matters is that you know your true nature and that you are at peace with your mind. Then, the time of death is also a time of

---

[29] Ajna chakra, located at the front of the head, between the eyebrows. Non-duality and Self-knowledge.
[30] Sahasrara chakra, crown of head, State of Presence, Self-Realisation.
[31] Jaideva Singh, ibid., p.95.
[32] The inner "yes" is not an obstacle to the outer "no".

liberation. *It is not the experience of enlightenment that counts but the state of your mind.* Yet, the experience of enlightenment has to be respected because it is the proof of an individual's genuine openness and understanding. Some people say "You are already enlightened. This is your natural state". Let us be clear. What is the natural state? Observe nature around. Is there anything more natural? Yet, would you say that nature is enlightened? For example, can you say that sunflowers are enlightened? Sunflowers are not enlightened, simply because they do not have a mind to realise their true nature. However, development and growth take place. Pure Consciousness is at the core of every form and allows the development of every form. When you are natural, ego does not influence you. Pure Consciousness is free to directly act through you. Like a flower, you are naturally conscious but you are not aware of it. In other words we can say, you are natural but you are not enlightened. The natural state is independent of enlightenment. Enlightenment happens when you are natural *and* you really understand who you are. You directly experience Truth (Pure Consciousness). Enlightenment is not a state. It is an experience that proves the realisation of the natural state. It is Grace because Light clears all shadows. There is no more ego programme. It is important to have clarity about enlightenment. Clarity puts an end to misunderstanding and confusion. Clarity also prevents the ego from playing with words, concepts, angles of perception and from claiming it is already enlightened. *You are*; but the paradox is that you can only realise who you are when you stop resisting who you are. This is self-integration (inner peace) and Self-knowledge.

Pure Consciousness is the true nature of everybody. But not everybody is conscious and open. It is not enough to intellectually understand oneness or non-duality. In actual life, you have to live it, *without pretence.* Your deeper self is already Pure Consciousness. Your true nature is Love. But given your belief system, can you really accept and manifest it? Liberation is the *true* opening to truth and love. "To know the Self is to be the Self".[33]

---

[33] Ramana Maharshi.

158

Do not be greedy for liberation, you will only remain bound. It is better not to worry about enlightenment. It comes when it has to come. The script is already written. The time is already known. Pay more attention to truth and have respect for general harmony. This is the surest and fastest way to open to the Heart and to be the Heart. Listen to your inner voice and you will not fall into any traps.

Myths and Traps

Some spiritual seekers come to the point of the Heart from the left (see the drawing): the progressive path. This is the inner path, the one of will power or devotion. The person with strong motivation may use very efficient methods (intense meditations, reciting mantras or powerful breathing exercises). There may be a feeling of being "high". One may go up very far vertically but forget to go down to the right and reconnect with the Heart (the point in the middle). The person going up very high or fast may experience difficult or deceptive states.

The Trap of Attraction for What is Extraordinary

Ego is attracted to what is extraordinary and usually rejects what is ordinary. This is how some people stray from the point and cannot open to the Heart. However, with understanding, they return Home: the inner space of openness and neutrality. From there, anything can be watched with detachment. An extraordinary state is not who you truly are and it is not something you should try to achieve. The Heart is totally neutral: a perfect point of balance, neither high nor low. When someone sees beauty only at the top floor of a building (emptiness) and not at the ground level (a big crowd), s/he cannot appreciate and embrace the totality of the construction. Both essence and existence need to be embraced.

On the inner path, the seeker may be trapped by some unusual experiences: hearing voices, seeing lights, having visions, feeling oneness or being in a state of bliss. Our true nature is like an infinite column. The higher realms lead to more extraordinary sensations and perceptions. The lower realms plunges us into the stories of the past without ever ending the purification process. However, it is again at the point of perfect balance between "heaven" and "earth": the point of the Heart, where you meet your true self.

By giving importance to unusual experiences, the ego may cling to them. The mind may no longer find the peace of the ordinary heart that simply accepts reality as it is.[34] No extraordinary events should divert your attention from what is "here and now". This means being grounded and listening to the heart. Only then can transformation happen naturally, without the interference of a personal will. The inner tree grows naturally step by step and in harmony with everything. Without ego, life, like nature, is simple and natural.

According to Ramana Maharshi, powers (siddhis) manifest mostly because of ego. However, there can be natural gifts. In the case of siddhis appearing spontaneously, he underlined the risk of getting attached to them and explained that such siddhis risk inflating the ego rather than eliminating it.[35] Extraordinary phenomena are not a problem. They can even become usual and ordinary. However, the excessive attraction and attention to "extraordinary" events is a trap. Keep your mind "here and now". Let it rest in the Heart. There, you do not pretend anything. You are humble and open to truth. You are not ambitious and greedy. You are not sophisticated and you are not attracted by power. Of course by being so simple, you may not be very interesting to some people. You may also be misunderstood. Do not pay attention to that. Be your true self.

Can you accept your ordinariness? Do you generally feel attracted and impressed by what is extraordinary? Can you accept being unnoticed? Can you let go of ideals or spiritual

---

[34] Rita Marie Robinson, *Ordinary Women Extraordinary Wisdom*, 2007, www.o-books.net.
[35] *Be As You Are. The Teachings of Sri Ramana Maharshi*, ibid., pp.156-160.

models? Open to truth and observe your clouds until they dissolve.

Pure Consciousness is the Heart. The innocence of the Heart is the supreme power. When you are detached from all powers, all powers surround you and manifest independently of your will.

Mental or Physiological Problems

If people try to force awakening while their personality is not integrated enough, they may experience psychological or physical problems. This is why it is better not to force anything. You have to be sufficiently reconciled with your ego beforehand. Some people feel resistance to or fears about engaging in spiritual practices. This has to be respected. Spiritual practices lead to more openness and receptivity to others. If the mind is still trapped in duality and non-acceptance, forcing the openness can create inner and mental disturbances.

Finally, some people are interested in finding peace of mind but they may neglect the body. This is also a sign that the mind is not fully integrated and balanced. Body and mind are interdependent. Respect your body as a temple of the Spirit. The outer world and the body are not mere illusions. They are manifested aspects of consciousness and in this sense, they are real and divine.

When the mind is not prepared for the opening (integrated enough), the body is not ready either. It may resist, shake, experience involuntary movements, sudden rises of energy (kundalini), strong heat or migraine headaches. People may also experience panic attacks and be confronted with their fears and inner demons (imaginary mental constructions or beliefs due to fears). Just as I was writing about this, I met someone who had this kind of experience. It is an interesting story to share. One day this man got confronted with his inner demons and he totally panicked. He even had to spend some time in a psychiatric hospital. When he came out, he started working on himself. After that, he once again experienced visions of demons all around him and coming through him. As he was no longer trying to resist them, the demons ended up laughing with him. This is a very beautiful story. I have heard a lot of spiritual awakening stories in which people go through phases of terror, fear of demons or extreme fear of dying. Some managed to overcome their fear by remembering that the fear of demons is an illusion. The mind imagines demons because it is afraid of truth and rejects some aspects of itself. I hope this story will encourage those having terrifying spiritual experiences, fear of others or fear of death, to just laugh at their own demons and overcome their fear. Who you truly are cannot die and cannot be affected. Detach from your fears. Do not take them seriously. Return to the Source.

The Trap of the Attachment to Peace

Natural peace does not depend upon outside conditions. One can live in the world and its "noise". The seekers whose peace is the result of isolation or techniques may believe they are firmly established in the Self while their ego leads them. It is easy to feel good in an air conditioned room but the outside temperature may be difficult to bear. People on the path of meditation may also sometimes be trapped by the flavour of silence and get attached to it. Of course, meditation helps to be in touch with inner peace. It is a precious tool to return to the Source, know and accept the mind, calm mental tendencies, taste the flavour of silence and in certain cases fully merge with it and realise the Self. However, if there is attachment to peaceful states, this will prevent natural peace.

Some people may have experiences of the void and define it as peace.[36] However, some experiences of the void may be the result of a lack of conscious connection to the Heart. Certain faces look very peaceful. Certain minds seem very silent but their silence is sometimes a silence of indifference. The Heart, though, is not indifferent. Being rooted in the Heart is the true silence of the mind.

---

[36] "Where the contraction or limitation of consciousness is predominant, there occurs knowership of the Void." Jaideva Singh, ibid., p.60.

162

This silence can also be expressed in the world, through words and amid the noise. It is independent of all this. When the mind is at peace, the outer world is not an obstacle. Those who are afraid of the outer world or of some kinds of people are afraid of themselves. This is why Self-realisation cannot happen. Of course, some people are truly at peace with themselves and wish to live in an isolated way. In this case, it is not because of fear or rejection. It is a free and natural choice.

Are you attached to peace or silence? Are you disturbed by certain individuals or by what is unexpected, noisy and different from what you are used to? If so, return to the Source. Observe your clouds until they dissolve.

Does your peace come from your mind or from your heart? Are you spontaneously open to everyone? When the cloud "fear of others" crosses your mind, watch it until it dissolves.

The Myth of the Absence of Thoughts

Self-realisation does not mean a total absence of thoughts. When a person has no more thoughts, it can be the result of techniques or isolation. This "silence" may have extraordinary effects (ecstasy, bliss, visions, siddhis, trance, no need for food) but sooner or later it will stop because the root of the flower has not yet been discovered. Do not interpret a temporary state of bliss as evidence of being enlightened. In Hindu terminology the state of no-thoughts is called "manolaya". More exactly it is a temporary stillness of thoughts. Ramana Maharshi said that: "Even if this temporary lulling of the mind should last a thousand years, it will never lead to total destruction of thought, which is what is called liberation from birth and death."[37] He added: "Due to the absence of a proper guide at this

---

[37] *Be As You Are. The Teachings of Sri Ramana Maharshi,* ibid., pp.59-60.

163

stage of spiritual practice, many have been deluded and fallen prey to a false sense of liberation."

The mind has to find its root in the Heart. From there, thoughts happen naturally. In some spiritual circles, some words may be banished, such as "thoughts", "desires" "judgments" or "anger." They are associated with ego. Actually, no words or actions should be banished. They all depend on the source from which they come. Simply observe whether the source of your thoughts, desires or anger is natural or mental. For example, anger can come from the Source (on the surface, you express anger because you feel it is the best solution in such circumstances but deep within, you remain peaceful). There is nothing to reject from the natural fruit. It is not conditioned. Your true nature expresses itself spontaneously. On the contrary, thoughts and desires are mental when they are conditioned by the past, guilt, fear, expectation and ambition.

Thoughts rising from the Source are not rooted in the past. They reveal a state of Presence. In this state, memory is less used. If you really want to make use of it, you can. You can still be efficient intellectually but the use of the intellect is no longer a regular function. When worries vanish, you are like a child who totally enjoys the present moment without thinking. Do not believe this is a loss. True universal intelligence operates through you. This is actually how the greatest discoveries are found.

The past does not have a strong impact when there is inner joy. Even when you get disturbed, the inner joy quickly returns. The past disappears. So think about nurturing your joy because it is what really allows you to go through different life experiences. Inner joy is what naturally brings you in a state of Presence. For example, do not try to be too perfect. This could be an obstacle to your joy and consequently, to the expression of your true perfection.

What makes you happy? Is it seeing a friend, eating sweets or ice cream, having a drink in a pub, smoking a cigar, eating a good meal, dancing all night, going to exquisite places, going shopping or staying at home? Just enjoy!

The Trap of Being Greedy for Awakening

Some people embark on a spiritual journey not to find peace and harmony but to awaken. They desire awakening for selfish reasons: their personal salvation or even in order to be a guru. They forget the Heart. What are the exact reasons that bring you on a spiritual path? Looking only for personal salvation makes no sense. Seeking truth, harmony and peace is a sign of a truly awakened life. Love is the only salvation. It is also the most direct way to receive divine Grace.

The Trap of External Dependence

Salvation and help can come from outside but the final key is in your hands. You can be guided and receive help. You can experience energetic openings. But the real opening has to come from your heart. If you remain dependent and greedy, if you cannot listen to your inner voice, if your mind is trapped in duality, separation, judgment, good and bad, you will not be able to realise your true nature. Simply trust your own self. Become a real and autonomous individual. Free your mind. Listen and open to your heart.

False Conceptions about Freedom

Some people think that being free is the supreme goal of spirituality. This depends though on how freedom is defined. Freedom without heart is but an illusion, certainly intoxicating but delusive. Real freedom is surrendering to the Heart. Love is the greatest freedom, beyond destiny.

False Conceptions about Attachment and Detachment

Misunderstandings about the concept of attachment may lead to unnatural detachments with unfortunate relational consequences. When the mind rests in the Heart, attachment and detachment do not mean anything. You can go beyond both by resisting neither one nor the other. True detachment comes from inner peace. If the situation you live is harmonious, do not be afraid of being attached to it. Fully enjoy your happiness! On the contrary, if there is no harmony, find the strength to detach. In this way, only the sense of harmony rules your life. Do not let the fear of attachment control you (otherwise you will be attached to detachment!) Also, do not believe that the fact of being married or having children is an obstacle. Who are you truly? Only false beliefs can prevent you from realising the Self.

On the other hand, if you are too detached and experience a certain lassitude of life, difficulties in being grounded and the feeling that you are leaving your body, try breathing into your belly to maintain the connection with the earth. When the natural time to leave your body comes, you will detach effortlessly and at peace with everybody.

The Myth of Sacrifice

Some spiritual seekers believe that in order to open to the Heart, they have to suffer and make sacrifices. Being your true self is an indication of happiness and blossoming. Listen to your heart. Do not force yourself. It knows your capacity and your limitations. It leads you to joy and harmony.

The Trap of the Lack of Understanding

Some people reach the Heart from the right (see drawing). It is the direct outer path, the natural way. It is more suitable for the people whose heart is sensitive. Guided by this sensitivity, these people

166

remain open in daily life and naturally integrate their ego. Thus, they can directly realise the Self, without previous psychological or physiological problems. However, there may be psychological disturbances afterwards. This is due to a lack of understanding of the new "opening".

When awakening happens spontaneously, it is natural to want to understand what it really means. However, this may be a trap if the mind gets caught in it. If the spiritual fire is not controlled, if the passion for the Divine does not diminish, one is like a live wire connected to a huge source of energy. It is then possible to lose mental balance. This is why it is said that the presence of a spiritual Master is generally necessary at a certain point.

At the beginning of my experience, my thirst for answers gave rise to many spiritual dreams. I kept on waking up in order to write everything down. I spent hours praying during the night. I was not eating much anymore. I was as if bewitched by the Divine. I saw signs everywhere, coincidences between my thoughts and external happenings. Everything seemed to echo and "talked" to me. I was less and less able to detach from this other plane of reality. These events of synchronicity were disturbing me. Little by little, the language and the words themselves took a different meaning. I automatically interpreted all speech in symbolic language, as if behind the words I could hear the true language. All language was transformed into word play. My mind wanted to interpret everything and gave it excessive attention. This was exhausting for me.

When there is self-doubt, excessive attention may be given to external signs. The mind needs to be reassured. It wants evidence. Yet, Truth can only be felt. It cannot be understood by the mind. It requires total trust in one's inner voice. Proof and confirmation only come when the trust in one's Self is total. Until doubt stops, truth naturally "shakes" the mind. Similarly, when truth manifests as a spiritual guide in your life, the whole structure of your mind and its belief system is questioned. The whole purpose of the "game" is to be yourself, to drop your mind and to trust your heart - *to be,* like a river which runs without stopping in spite of rocks and obstacles, a natural stream which inevitably joins with the ocean. One fine day, the eyes see the "Ocean" and understand its mystery. Both the heart and the mind are conscious and merge. The opening to the Self is totally conscious.

The Trap of Comparison

The person coming to the Heart from the left (see drawing), has a background of meditation, contemplation or absorption of the mind. This person looks like a nice smooth apple that received excellent nutrients to grow. The mind is steady but it may still be ambitious. The priority may be given to freedom and not to love. Also, there may be a feeling of superiority because the spiritual ego feeds on its detachment, experiences or "achievements". Finally there may be the tendency to self-protect, a feeling that one's purity needs to be safeguarded. The mind does not yet rest in the Heart to embrace reality as it is. However, when this "fruit" opens to the Heart (welcomes its ego as spiritually ambitious, selfish, arrogant and in need of protection), it is impressive. The mind is already steady and clear. Mental tendencies are mastered. This is the "fruit of the heavens".

The person coming to the point of the Heart from the right (see drawing), has had many experiences in life and managed to keep an open Heart. Just like an organic apple, there may be marks on the peel but the taste is good. The Heart is strong. The "organic apple" does not look impressive because it is natural. It can reach the Heart and "open the door" without yet being the complete master of the mind. But this fruit is used to all kinds of winds and is able to go through many storms. It matures slowly but safely to find clarity and mastery of mind. This is the natural "fruit of the earth".

The "organic apple" may have doubts about itself because it does not look like the "supermarket one". It may think that it should resemble a smooth and unblemished apple. In trying to do so, it risks moving away from its naturalness: its real jewel. The common belief deceiving many spiritual seekers is that only very smooth fruits are

Divine. Being in a state of bliss, of super-consciousness, being absolutely calm and silent, are considered signs of "spiritual success". However, these beliefs limit your potential to directly open to the Self.

It is important to free yourself from ideals and spiritual myths because they prevent you from simply being yourself, with all your colours. Ego imperfections are fine, as long as you acknowledge them. Awakening is beyond perfection and imperfection, beyond high and low. It is not found by plunging into subtler and subtler spheres of consciousness, nor by paying too much attention to past stories and the "wounds" of the earth. Enlightenment is at the point of balance between heaven and earth. This is the point of acceptance and integration: the Heart.

"Humane sentiments, compassion, an intuitive interconnectedness and selflessness are the foundational elements of true spirituality". [38] You can be awakened and still be very human. You may cry, feel fragile, feel pain, have the same ego tendencies as everybody else but unlike most people you do not resist them. This is why they eventually cease to influence you. The fledgling bird does not seek to grow. It just grows, naturally. One day, the bird opens its wings towards the infinite space. Trying to reach the sky before opening your wings is a delusion. So keep accepting your ego as it is "here and now" and through self-acceptance, open to the infinite space.

The Trap of Receptivity and the Mirror Effect

The more the mind opens, the more the boundaries between oneself and others disappear. This can be disturbing if the open person (awakened or not) does not understand what is happening or does not know him/herself well enough. For many years before my experience I found it strange to be so changeable depending on the people I was with. With some I laughed about everything, with others I could not

[38] Akhand Jyoti magazine, The Light Divine, May-June 2010, p.42, vol. 8, Issue: 3. Thank you Annamalai.

laugh. Sometimes, I was very talkative and sometimes, I had nothing to say. I would feel very different inner states, some of them unusual and occasionally disturbing. Luckily, I could still accept them all. I never paid too much attention to them because inside me there was a force that could "digest" and absorb them: a generally happy nature. However, sometimes, I would feel strange. Who am I really? Some inner states did not seem to be my natural self. What was all of that about?

Over the years, I became aware of what was really happening. One day, a personal experience finally proved to me that some inner emotions did not pertain to "me". They were the result of my openness. I was simply receptive to the energy of the person in front of me or receptive to people's thoughts. It was such a relief to understand this and to finally have proof that I could not question. Until then, I had doubted myself, thinking that all the inner states I was feeling were "me". People who are very receptive can easily understand what a relief it is to finally have clarity on this issue. Tears were running from my eyes. I could now detach from the ego. This awareness really lifted the inner burden.

The inner nature of someone receptive does not change but it can be temporarily different. Sometimes, the receptive person may even say words that simply reflect the thoughts of others. In certain cases, it may take a little while for one's energy to get back to its usual natural self. Because the receptive person is a mirror, s/he may be misjudged. If this is the case for you, keep trusting your divine force. Remind yourself that clouds come and disappear. In the process, some people get the chance to look into the mirror and see their own reflection...When someone's ego projects a film on a screen, the screen looks like the film. [39] But the screen is not the film. This phenomenon of projection allowed me to understand two points. The first one is that the signs which are sometimes considered significant to confirm an opinion can actually be meaningless. Therefore, it is

---

[39] Similarly, numerology proves that 9+1 becomes 1 (9+1=10=1+0=1). With 9, the result is always equal to the added number.

important to detach from personal beliefs and signs, even if they appear true. It is better to rely on your inner voice only. Follow your intuition. Do not trust your mind. The second point is that whenever you feel strange feelings about a person, you should try to get clarity about the situation as soon as possible. However, if communication is not possible or if the situation remains unclear or ambiguous, it is better to keep some distance or to keep quiet. In any case, all projections, all hasty judgments you may have about others are always learning experiences because they are often keys to freedom - mirrors of the limitations, fears and aspects of the ego that you reject.

It is now time to really remember your true identity and not to forget it again. Identify with this: "I am not the ego. I am the Presence that includes the ego as well as everything else". Just as the wind rises and disappears, everything that manifests and disappears on the screen of consciousness has only a relative reality. Do not identify with the wind, with what is fleeting (body, thoughts and emotions). Identify with that which is the Source of all forms and which cannot be affected: Pure Consciousness. Remember that within all forms, Pure Consciousness is like the open eyes of a child. Forms and Pure Consciousness are in perfect symbiosis. The movie and the screen are One. With understanding, oneness can be appreciated for what it really is: completely meeting others, which is also completely meeting your true Self (inside and outside). This brings renewal, stability and joy.

This receptive and mirror phenomenon also concerns children, as they are open and innocent. It is important to understand young children and be very reassuring as they may experience strong emotions. They should not feel guilty. It is natural to feel and express emotions. Throughout their childhood, they need to be comforted, to hear that their true nature is perfectly good and to understand that we had the same "problems" at their age. This really helps them to lift the burden of having to be perfect or different from their present condition. Whether it is our own children or the children of others, let us accept without judging the stages they go through (attachment, jealousy, shyness, anger, tears, preferences for certain friends,

171

activities and clothes). Every stage is temporary. This respect for natural stages helps children stay in direct contact with their true nature and joy.

Respecting children is also teaching them to respect others. For this, boundaries sometimes need to be set. It is important to be firm (with love). Children's behaviour needs to be corrected when the situation requires. But this can be done without sticking any negative and definitive labels on them: "You are like this or like that". It is equally important to be reassuring. Children have to regularly hear that our scolding them does not mean that they are "bad". They need to be reminded that they are always truly good and that we love them the way they are. Correcting their behaviour from time to time is simply natural. It is also natural, as parents or educators, to occasionally make mistakes. As long as we give children love, small mistakes are not important.

Let us not compare: "Your sister or brother were like this and you are not." Each child is unique and truly beautiful. Let us not judge our children. Instead, let us adapt to their behaviour. Children are all different and evolve at their own rhythm. They show by their behaviour what we should do and when limits have to be set (e.g. if it is the time to detach a little bit or to be very present because this is what they need). Let us follow our intuition and give them love. Love is all that counts.

If they do not feel "good", help them again to understand that they are always truly good. If their mind tells them some silly stories, they should not feel bad. Thoughts are not who they are! Who they truly are is always perfect. Thoughts are simply like clouds in the sky. Like clouds, negative thoughts come and disappear. It is natural to have them sometimes. The distinction between their true self (space) and thoughts (clouds) helps children not to feel guilty and to integrate their true identity. Children need to know who they really are because they feel it inside. Then, there is no problem and no duality.

Children can also become the friends of their fears. Fears are temporary thoughts only. When they look at a cloud in the sky, it quickly dissolves. Similarly, when they see that their fear is nothing

172

other than a little cloud in the mind, it disappears. "There is no danger". If some fears persist, let them imagine a bag where they can put all their fears after naming them. Then they can throw the bag away. This can be done as often as needed, until all fears disappear.

They also need to understand that their spirit is like space. It never dies. Can space disappear? Space cannot die and it flows through everything. It caresses every flower. It flutters about with the butterflies. It plays with all sorts of animals. It glides with the eagle and it dances with the leaves in the wind. Their spirit is like space and also like love: it has no boundaries. It is One with everything and everybody. *We are always together*. There is no reason to worry. The body is like a coat that we put on at the time of birth and that we naturally remove one day because it is the time to join with the infinite space and to fly with the bird... May the joy of each child be like an eternal flame.

The Trap of Identifying with the Spiritual Person

By identifying with the spiritual person or the teacher, spontaneity may be lost or exaggerated. It may also be less easy to recognise certain ego tendencies or to admit some weaknesses (e.g. taking yourself seriously, comparing, having a feeling of superiority, forgetting to be grateful to the people who have helped you). Then, the game may continue, this time under the cover of authenticity. This would be a subtle and deceptive game.

As long as you doubt yourself, you feel the need to prove your spiritual identity. Be very vigilant concerning this. Self-doubt can take subtle and "divine" forms. For example, you may wish to fulfil a divine mission. You may also believe you are an instrument or a servant of Divine Consciousness when you are actually only lead by your ego. Return to the Source. Who wants this? Is it your true nature (uncontaminated by fears, selfish desires, the need for security, the need to prove and to be loved) or is it the ego (conditioned by those very same things)? Is your spiritual activity the result of a natural movement to share or the effect of your pride or ambition? One needs first to open to truth to really guide others. It is only when one has self-mastery (of one's selfish desires and fears) that one can truly be a Master for others. Of course, you can very well have something to share and do so with sincerity, without playing any role and pretending anything. In this case, ego is not active. What you share comes from a place of truth. Truth opens the door. Pretence closes it. Choose Truth.

Teaching or sharing one's understanding is natural. As long as there is ignorance, the Heart *naturally* wishes to help, but without expecting results. Naturally, parents help their children to become happy and respectful adults. Teaching also happens by itself when there is a true intention to help. Then, circumstances, events and experiences of life all contribute to the content of the teaching. The Heart does its teaching independently of everything. It is done through thousands of people around. This teacher is in everything and everything is in it. This teacher is in you and all around you. Have trust. It is your inner friend, your inner child, your innocence and it is also existence itself.

Your guide and your protector are already inside you, as well as around you. The five natural elements (nature) are inside and outside of you. Gods and Goddesses are eternally present. Knowledge is within you. All answers already exist. Connect with your inner friend through silence, contemplation, prayers, dancing or chanting. Ask for help or answers and they will be provided (if you really need them). Follow also your intuition to know which spiritual path corresponds to you. All spiritual paths are perfect, as long as they suit you and bring about peace and harmony. Let us respect all our differences in belief, religion, ritual and expression of the Divine.

Natural Roses Blossom

By listening to the Heart, one fine day, inevitably, the Child returns Home. The river joins with the Ocean...Love...so vast and magnificent...

See my friend the Orient, the Occident, duality, wrong, correct,
All merging into the Source beyond bounds and defects.
It pulls you to the stream,
Where you can rejoice and dream.
Embrace the beauty, feel the caress of the wind.
It is such a dream, such a reality, a mystery, although a true scene,
Eternally there for you as a gift so you can be called.
Listen my friend, listen to the call of your inner Child.
This is your everlasting shelter, untouched and mild.

Peace, Love and Joy to all beings.

www.ingramcontent.com/pod-product-compliance
Lightning Source LLC
Chambersburg PA
CBHW052002090426
42741CB00008B/1514